ARTISTS OF THE NATIONAL LIBRARY OF AUSTRALIA

ELLIS ROWAN

With an essay by Patricia Fullerton

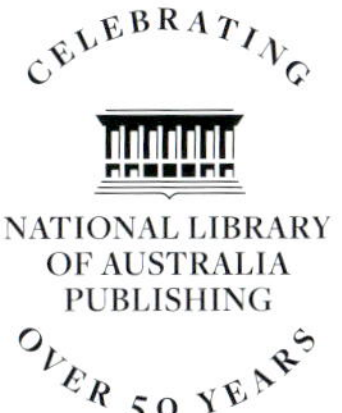

Published by National Library of Australia Publishing
Canberra ACT 2600

ISBN: 9781922507662

© National Library of Australia 2024

The National Library of Australia acknowledges Australia's First Nations Peoples—the First Australians—as the Traditional Owners and Custodians of this land and gives respect to the Elders—past and present—and through them to all Australian Aboriginal and Torres Strait Islander people.

This book is copyright in all countries subscribing to the Berne Convention. Apart from any fair dealing for the purpose of research and study, criticism or review, as permitted under the *Copyright Act 1968*, no part may be reproduced by any process without written permission. Enquiries should be made to the publisher.

Publisher: Lauren Smith
Managing editor: Amelia Hartney
Designer: Stan Lamond
Image coordinator: Madeleine Warburton

Printed in China by Asia Pacific Offset on FSC®-certified paper.

Find out more about NLA Publishing at nla.gov.au/national-library-publishing.

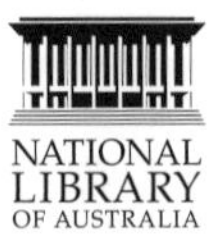

A catalogue record for this book is available from the National Library of Australia

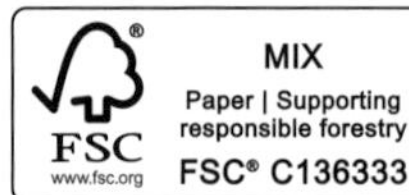

Foreword

In 2002, the National Library of Australia, with Patricia Fullerton, curated the exhibition *The Flower Hunter: Ellis Rowan*, introducing a new audience to these beautiful large-scale paintings of birds and flowers and the intrepid woman who painted them. Early in my Library career, I was one of those discovering her work for the first time.

In her lifetime, Ellis Rowan's work received international recognition. She exhibited nationally and internationally to great acclaim, winning many medals. She gifted three of her works to Queen Victoria. In 1920, she exhibited 1,000 of her works in Sydney. So well known was she that the Australian Government agreed to acquire a significant collection of her works—although there was some haggling over the price before it was acquired in 1923.

The National Library is proud to be the custodian of that collection of 919 watercolours and gouaches painted between 1870 and 1920. Together with her personal papers and a childhood journal—donated by her niece Lady Casey, in 1956 and 1968—as well as her own memoir, they reveal the life and artistic output of a woman who travelled the world, ignoring the advice of many, and created her own path. Whether it be in London, Australia or Papua New Guinea, Ellis Rowan was not a woman to let family ties, the advice of men or corsets and long skirts get in her way.

Since that exhibition, people have continued to fall in love with Rowan's work. It is always represented in the Library's Treasures Gallery. It has been reproduced on gift cards, wrapping paper, calendars and in an exquisite collection designed by Australian fashion house Zimmermann.

This book reproduces the works displayed in the 2002 exhibition, as well as 21 other works in the National Library's collection, alongside Patricia Fullerton's curator's essay. It will introduce Rowan to a new generation of flower hunters and art lovers. And once you have enjoyed her in these pages, there is more Ellis Rowan to discover in the National Library's digital collections.

Kathryn Favelle
Director, Reader Services, National Library of Australia
Canberra, 2024

Introduction

Petite, plucky and always immaculately dressed in the constraint of Victorian finery, for almost 50 years Ellis Rowan explored the world in search of exotic flowers and wildlife to paint. Today, over 3,000 works in major public and private collections testify to her prodigious output and her determination to record as many, until then unknown, specimens—many of which have since become endangered or extinct.

Most of Ellis Rowan's original watercolour studies on grey paper were executed under extreme difficulties: in the heat of the dusty desert, pestered by flies or in the humid conditions of a tropical rainforest where snakes and crocodiles lurked. She worked quickly, and often on site. Her powers of observation, compositional skill, sense of colour, deftness with the brush and natural facility of technique without any preliminary sketch were without compromise.

Throughout her life she was acclaimed internationally, winning 29 medals, and accolades from leading art critics. Her work was also collected by royalty, including Queen Victoria. Few painters in the history of Australian art have been so honoured; yet it is hard to think of any who have been so maligned, particularly by male artists, in an ongoing debate on the merit of her work in the 80 years since her death. It is not simply that Ellis Rowan was a woman working in a field dominated by men; her subject-matter isolated her from the landscapists and figure painters of the day, as did her embrace of the 'Art for Art's Sake' movement, which valued all things decorative, including the painting of screens and murals, designs for porcelain, illustrations for books and magazines, and other creative areas, including writing.

Marian Ellis Rowan (nee Ryan) was born in Melbourne on 30 July 1848, the eldest of seven children of pioneering parents, Charles and Marian Ryan. Her father had emigrated from Kilfera, County Kilkenny, Ireland, in 1840, taking a lease at *Kilfera Station,* some 120 kilometres north of Melbourne in the Port Phillip District, then part of the colony of New South Wales.

Her mother was the eldest daughter of the English naturalist and ornithologist John Cotton, who emigrated with his wife and nine children in 1843, taking up several properties on the Goulburn and Broken Rivers, including *Doogallook,* not far from Charles Ryan.[1] Although Ellis Rowan was a baby at the time of her grandfather's death, she inherited his sketchbooks as well as his botanical interest and artistic ability.[2]

By the time of John Cotton's death in 1849, Charles Ryan had already leased *Killeen Station* at Longwood, near the Strathbogie Ranges, where the young Ellis Rowan spent her early childhood. In 1853, Ryan set up a successful business in Melbourne. Ellis Ryan attended Miss Murphy's refined school, taking subjects required for a young Victorian lady: scripture, French, English history, singing, the art of embroidery, lace-making and painting in watercolour.

In 1869, aged 21, Rowan made her first trip abroad, basing herself in England for a year. Her uncle was the Royal Academician Sir Charles Eastlake, so she would have had every opportunity to avail herself of London's artistic circles. On her return, a 'Miss Ellis Ryan' won a bronze medal for a screen with four panels of Australian wildflowers, at the Intercolonial Exhibition in Melbourne in 1872.

Whatever her botanical interests had been, they would have expanded when her father, a keen botanist himself, bought 26 acres on Mount Macedon. *Derriweit Heights* commanded one of the best views on the mountain. It was a typical colonial hill-station with an internationally famous garden. Ferdinand von Mueller, the government botanist, advised on exotic plants from around the world, and the garden layout was designed by W.R. Guilfoyle.

The house looked down over a sloping lawn, where Guilfoyle used a mountain stream to create five lakes. Covered in waterlilies and bordered by ferns, clumps of New Zealand flax, with groves of silver birches and Japanese maples to provide dappled shade, the lakes became one of the great features of *Derriweit Heights*. Rhododendrons were planted under exotic trees, as well as foxgloves, violets and gentians along the shady paths that led from one level of the garden to

1 Before arriving in Australia, John Cotton had published two books on English birds and had intended to write and illustrate another on the birds of the Port Phillip District before he died in 1849, aged 47. It was subsequently published by M. Casey: *John Cotton's Birds of the Port Phillip District of New South Wales 1843–1849* (Melbourne: William Collins, 1974).

2 Ellis Rowan was not the only member of the family to devote her life to depicting and preserving nature. Her brother Charles became a famous doctor and hero of the 1870s Turkish wars, and later a founding member of the Royal Australian Ornithologists Union. Her cousins, the Le Souefs, established the first zoos in Melbourne, Sydney and Perth. Her aunt, Caroline (nee Cotton), painted decorative boxes containing miniature Aboriginal weapons carved by her husband Albert Le Souef.

another, creating a series of 'bosky dells' and colourful displays set against the Australian bush background, where koalas and platypus abounded.[3]

Through her father's collaboration with von Mueller, Rowan was invited to contribute botanical studies for his comprehensive collection of Australian flora in anticipation of a publication on the subject.[4] Von Mueller's bold handwriting appears on the back of many of her pictures identifying the subjects in botanical Latin. He encouraged her work and gave her useful introductions to key people around the world. They kept in touch until his death in 1896.

In June 1873, Ellis Ryan became engaged to Captain Frederic Charles Rowan, an officer in the British army. Frederic Rowan had spent several years in England undergoing facial reconstruction after being wounded in the New Zealand Maori Wars, before returning via Melbourne to become Sub-Inspector for the Constabulary of Armed Forces in New Zealand. Four months after meeting, they celebrated their marriage at the Ryan family home in Richmond, before settling in New Zealand at Pukearuhe on the North Island. Living as an officer's wife, isolated from friends and family, Rowan found the domesticity of married life 'boring'; but, ever resourceful, and under her husband's exacting eye and encouragement, she applied herself to painting local wildflowers. Years later in New York she recalled: 'Long into the night, longing to give up, to give in, sometimes with tears running down my face, I worked to please him'.[5]

In January 1875, Ellis Rowan returned to her family home in Macedon, where she painted for six months awaiting the birth of her only child, Frederic Charles Eric Elliott Rowan, known simply as Puck. They spent the next three years in New Zealand before Frederic Rowan returned to Australia in 1878 to establish himself and his family in the thriving business world of Melbourne, the most prosperous city in Australasia. Through his influential connections, Frederic Rowan was able to assist his wife's career; he was a member of the board of *The Picturesque Atlas of Australasia,* which, in 1886, published illustrations by Ellis Rowan and other known artists.[6]

---

3 M. Hazzard and H. Hewson, *Flower Paintings of Ellis Rowan from the Collection of the National Library of Australia* (Canberra: National Library of Australia, 1982), p. 33. *Derriweit Heights* was razed to the ground in the bush-fires of 1983.

4 It was von Mueller's great disappointment that he had to hand over his botanical work to Sir Joseph Hooker, Director of the Royal Botanic Gardens in Kew, for a collaboration with George Bentham, resulting in the publication of *Flora Australiensis (1863–1878)* in seven volumes. See H. Hewson, *Australia: 300 Years of Botanical Illustration* (Melbourne: CSIRO Publishing, 1999), p. 130.

5 *New York Times,* 16 January 1898.

6 A. Carran (ed.), *Australia: The First Hundred Years* (Sydney: The Picturesque Atlas Publishing Company Ltd., 1886; reprinted Sydney: Paul Hamlyn, 1978).

As the corporate wife, Rowan accompanied her husband on his energetic business trips around Australia, taking the opportunity to paint indigenous flowers wherever she could. On her initial trips to Adelaide and Western Australia, she painted delicate bouquets of mixed wildflowers, which she exhibited for the first time under her married name, 'Mrs F.C. Rowan', at the Sydney International Exhibition in 1879, winning a silver medal.

In October 1880, the Melbourne Exhibition Building opened in style, attracting exhibits from 30 countries and the six Australian colonies, with 32,000 samples of produce and culture. Here Rowan first incurred the indignation of her fellow painters when she won a gold medal for a four-leaved screen on satin and special merit for ten framed groups of New Zealand wildflowers on satin.[7] Members of the Victorian Artists' Society protested to the jurors, who stuck by their decision, but later, begrudgingly, conceded a silver medal to Louis Buvelot, the highly esteemed painter of the Australian landscape. Rowan ignored the petty squabblings and competitive jealousy of the art world and set about discovering new flowers to paint for von Mueller.

On one of her many trips with her husband, in 1880, Rowan met the lone English painter Marianne North, at Albany on the south coast of Western Australia. North included birds, butterflies, fungi and insects in her paintings, as much for their intrinsic interest as to show their role in the ecological balance of nature. She was an inspiration to Rowan. Twenty-five years later Rowan recalled:

> *I became her devoted admirer, and she became the pioneer of my ambition. A world-wide traveller in search of specimens, her description of her adventures was so vivid, so graphic, so thrilling in its prospects of wider fields that I became infected, stimulated by an example and a result beyond dreams successful* [8]

In March 1883, leaving her husband and eight-year-old son, and armed with introductions, Rowan travelled with her sister Blanche Ryan to England via Ceylon and India, where she painted in the Himalayan foothills. At the Intercolonial Exhibition in Calcutta her works were compared

7 Rowan's four-leaved screen 'was the most prominent feature of attraction. It consists of beautiful arrangements of native flowers of Victoria, New Zealand and New South Wales, executed in water colours upon black, pale yellow, pale blue and crimson satin'. *Official Record, Melbourne International Exhibition 1880–1881* (Melbourne: Commissioners, Mason, Firth and McCutcheon, 1882), p. 427; Hazzard, op. cit., p. 38.

8 Ellis Rowan, 'An Australian Artist's Adventures', *New Idea*, 6 February 1905, p. 714.

with the new art form of photography: 'There are a dozen watercolours in the Victorian Court, of the indigenous wildflowers of Australia ... which in point of excellence, of execution, beauty of colouring and artistic grouping ... are worth all the photographs in the exhibition put together'.[9] That year Rowan won gold medals in Amsterdam, St Petersburg and Calcutta, and the following year one for lace-making in Denmark, shortly after her husband had been appointed Danish consul in Melbourne.

By the winter of 1887, Rowan made the first of six trips to Queensland. Overwhelmed by the luscious colour and succulence of the tropical vegetation, she did some of her best paintings in dazzling colour and startling composition, which were duly recognised the following year when she scooped the awards at the 1888 Centennial International Exhibition, in particular for her large oil paintings *Chrysanthemums* and *Marguerites*.

There was a storm of protest. Members of the Victorian Artists' Society called a meeting to contest the judgement, as they had done eight years before, penning an indignant letter of protest. In response, the jury not only confirmed its decision, but also ridiculed the insolence of the Society and the signatories, John Mather and George Ashton, and their attempts 'to injure the artistic reputation of the lady overtly referred to in the resolution'.[10] Although this was a major triumph for Rowan, the bitterness of her male rivals was permanent and they continued to spurn and ridicule her work long after her death, contributing to the difficulty of later finding a lasting home for her paintings.[11]

Ellis Rowan was now the most recognised painter in Australia and was rapidly becoming a household name. The following year, in 1889, she went on to win five first prizes and a gold medal at the Adelaide Jubilee Exhibition and her success, as well as her social connections, led to commissions in oils. She painted murals at her cousin Lady Janet Clarke's house *Cliveden*, murals in the governor's dining room at the Victorian Racing Club and, even more unlikely for a

9 *The Calcutta Englishman*, Calcutta, 27 November 1893.
10 *Argus*, Melbourne, 25 January 1889; Hazzard, op. cit., p. 51.
11 Tom Roberts refused to acknowledge her presence when they met on Murray Island, north of Cape York, in 1892. See Ellis Rowan, *The Flower Hunter: The Adventures in Northern Australia and New Zealand of Flower Painter Ellis Rowan* (Sydney: Angus and Robertson, 1991), p. 130; and McKay, *Ellis Rowan: A Flower-Hunter in Queensland* (Brisbane: Queensland Museum, 1990), p. 24–26. As late as 1935, Roberts' friend Arthur Streeton wrote that his painting *Spring Pastoral* had been restored by 'amateur hands (Mrs Ellis Rowan)' (*The Arthur Streeton Catalogue*. Melbourne: Arthur Streeton, 1935, p. 114). Now in the collection of the National Gallery of Victoria, this painting was displayed as a key work at the opening of Federation Square in Melbourne.

woman at the time, in 1893, she painted 12 large oil panels for the walls of The Australian Club, the prestigious men's club in Melbourne.[12]

Rowan returned to the tropical warmth of Queensland during the winters of 1891 and 1892, claiming a need to escape for her health. Captivated by the variety of the lush tropical vegetation, she sent 65 paintings back to von Mueller for identification. The exaggerated letters describing her adventures to her husband Frederic Rowan form the first part of her autobiography:

> *My first walk in the wild tropical jungle ... I cannot forget. I entered, sketchbook in hand, by a narrow little pathway, probably made by an alligator. I kicked, as I thought, a grey stick aside—it was a snake, and quick as lightning it darted off, while I grew hot and cold in turns ... A few steps farther on I came to an opening, and below me lay a miniature lake, its water covered with large blue lilies floating amid their leaves on which the sun shone through a network of graceful palms. Scarlet, yellow-eyed dragonflies skimmed over its surface, while presently a great butterfly tremulously fluttered past, and the sunlight, catching the metallic lustre of its wings, changed them to every rainbow hue.*[13]

Her tales of near disaster fully satisfied her lust for adventure. She suffered bruises, a black eye and the occasional fever, complained of stinging nettles, mosquito bites and sunburn. Amongst other things in her quest, she dangled by ropes over precipices, defied turbulent seas, a bolting horse and a hair-raising trip by rail.

Her return to Melbourne in December 1892 coincided with her husband's sudden death at 47. Although they had spent much of their life apart, Frederic Rowan had fully supported her career throughout their marriage, and they had shared an intimacy in their letters and expectations of each other. The young widow, now in her mid-forties, made her home permanently at *Derriweit Heights*.[14] After a short period of grieving, Rowan began her travels again with a new sense of

---

12 The 12 panels at The Australian Club are of various subjects ranging from waterlilies to tropical palms, painted on butcher's paper and attached to the walls by an embossed gold border. No photographs are known of her wall decoration at *Cliveden*, but a photograph of one of her screens *in situ* is reproduced in A. Montana, *The Art Movement in Australia: Design, Taste and Society 1875–1900* (Melbourne: Miegunyah Press, 2000), p. 153. A photograph of her murals at the Victorian Racing Club Dining Room can be seen at the Australian Racing Museum, Caulfield (VRMI 1795).

13 Rowan, op. cit., 1991, p. 12.

14 The economic depression of the early 1890s caused bankruptcy and ruin for many Melbourne businessmen, including Rowan's father. As much as Charles Ryan fought the prospect of bankruptcy, in 1896 he was eventually forced to sell his beloved *Derriweit Heights*, moving his remaining family into the small gardener's cottage on the property.

freedom, revisiting New Zealand the following year on a lengthy trip covering both the North and South Islands. During her travels, she painted black-and-white landscapes, which were reproduced in *The Town and Country Journal* in December 1893, with a serialised account of her trip. Her adventure-packed letters to her family form the second part of her autobiography. That same year, in 1893, she entered what was to be her last international competition, exhibiting 99 paintings in the World Columbian Exhibition in Chicago. She won a gold medal.[15]

In 1895, Ellis Rowan embarked on a trip to England that was to take her away from Australia for some ten years. Through the connections of her younger brother Cecil Ryan and armed with a large number of paintings, Rowan made contact with royalty. Within days of her visit, she received a letter from Windsor Castle: 'The Queen has seen your paintings and ... was much pleased with them ... [and] has kept three. These the Queen will have made into a screen for her own room and there they will prove not only most ornamental but most useful to Her Majesty'.[16]

The following year, in 1896, Ellis Rowan staged her first solo show outside Australia, exhibiting 100 paintings of Australian wildflowers at the fashionable Dowdeswell Galleries in New Bond Street, Mayfair. At the private viewing on 20 April 1896, the Queen's cousin, the Duchess of Teck, opened the show and bought three paintings for herself. The papers were filled with descriptions of the glittering occasion and many glowing reviews, including one by the eminent ex-President of the Royal Academy Lord Leighton: 'Mrs Rowan's work is characterised by exquisite purity of tone without feebleness, and the most brilliant colour without harshness—each specimen botanically perfect ... created into a lovely picture'.[17] Ellis Rowan had become a good ambassador for her country and her work sold well, resulting in commissions for murals and oil paintings in prestigious addresses around London, including 13 panels for Lord Newton's house in Belgrave Square.[18]

Rowan next set her sights on America. Equipped with introductions, she set off for a visit, which lasted more than seven years. In New York, she met the young botanist Alice Lounsberry

---

15 In the same competition, Tom Roberts and A.H. Fullwood won awards for oils; Lister Lister, Fullwood and Ellis Rowan for watercolours.

16 Letter to Ellis Rowan from Windsor Castle, 17 May 1895. In her cuttings book, Rowan pasted the telegram from Windsor Castle on the opening page (Manuscripts Collection, National Library of Australia (MS2206)).

17 Rowan later claimed that Lord Leighton said her collection was unique and valued it at £15,000 (see *Queenslander*, 10 June 1911). See also J. McKay, 'Ellis Rowan, a Flower Hunter', *Art in Australia*, vol. 27, Winter 1990, p. 579. Leighton's praise was later included in the publicity generated for Rowan's 1920 travelling exhibition to America (see Manuscripts Collection, National Library of Australia (MS806)). See also Hazzard, op. cit., p. 112.

18 *The British Australian*, 4 January 1896. For further reviews see Hazzard, op. cit., p. 88–90.

and together, over four years, they travelled through the United States and the West Indies, collaborating on three books that became standard texts for botany students: *A Guide to the Wildflowers* (1899), *A Guide to the Trees* (1900) and *Southern Wildflowers and Trees* (1901).[19]

After completing her work with Lounsberry, she continued to travel and paint throughout the United States, and held several exhibitions at prestigious venues. During the first months of her visit to California for the 1904 Panama-Pacific Exposition at Stanford University, she learned of the deaths of her father and also of her son Puck, who died tragically aged 22 in a gaol in Mashonaland, Zimbabwe, where he may have been involved with the Australian cavalry during the Boer War.[20] Sometime after hearing the news, she underwent a transformation with experimental surgery on her face. This 'face-lift', a new American fad, gave her, what one reporter described as, 'the look of a sad monkey in a small childish face'.[21] She dyed her hair red with henna and reduced her said-age by ten years.

Records suggest Rowan returned to Australia towards the end of 1904. In 1906, she once again turned to the remote and inhospitable parts of Australia as a focus for her work, making a foray to the goldmining area of Kalgoorlie, Laverton and Goongarrie in Western Australia. Despite her incongruous appearance, dressed in a long white skirt, nipped in at the waist by a sash, with gloves and veil, the local people regarded her with respect. She in turn again claimed her passion for Western Australian flora, stating that some of the most beautiful flowers were found in the sandhills near Laverton.

Although Ellis Rowan was looking for a major buyer for her entire collection, a number of key purchases of her works were made during this time. The South Australian Government bought 80 works for £500 from a much-acclaimed Adelaide exhibition.[22] Some of these were a collection of wildflower paintings from a trip Rowan made to Broken Hill in time to capture a rich red carpet of Sturt's Desert peas in full bloom. Sir John Downer, the politician and supporter of women's rights, bought 20 works, which today are housed in the South Australian Herbarium at the Botanical Gardens in Adelaide. The Sydney Technical College bought 65 paintings

---

19 A new colour printing process is described in the preface to Alice Lounsberry, *A Guide to the Wild Flowers* (New York: Frederick A. Stokes and Co., 1899), with its 64 coloured and 100 black-and-white plates. Rowan had 12 paintings from that publication made into a portfolio for sale at US$5.00. In 1980, one of these folios sold in Melbourne for $1,200 (see Hazzard, op. cit. p. 98).
20 Hazzard, op. cit., p. 97.
21 Ibid, p. 104.
22 At the Society Art Rooms, North Terrace.

from an exhibition at Angus and Robertson Gallery in Sydney; these paintings are now in the Powerhouse Museum. In her hometown Melbourne, Rowan is today represented by five works in the National Gallery of Victoria, one of which, *Pandorea jasminoides,* is rated a public favourite in the collection.

After her exhibition at the Old Town Hall in Brisbane in August 1912, the Queensland Government bought 100 paintings for £1,000. Rowan gave an extra 25 works for £50, making a total of 125 works, which today are housed in the Queensland Museum. The political groundwork that Rowan had put into securing this deal was widely publicised in the press and opened up the debate as to whether her works should be represented as art in a gallery or as botanical studies in a museum. While Rowan was finally beginning to find permanent homes for some of her work, her battle for securing her major collection for posterity was yet to come.

In May 1916 and in the middle of the Great War, Ellis Rowan, now 68 years old, set off to the new Australian protectorate of New Guinea for seven months, on commission to paint 100 flowers and some birds of paradise for fine china importers Flavelle Brothers. The flower paintings from this trip were nothing like the delicate posies of her youth—they had become overwhelmingly luscious, oozing off the edge of the paper, and confrontingly bold in colour.

When she returned to Sydney, welcomed back like a national treasure, Rowan told reporters flocking to interview her, that she had every intention of returning to New Guinea: 'I found the most marvellous flowers quite close at hand, the most wonderful flowers in the whole world ... I am the first person to paint these flowers—the first white person indeed to see any of them'.[23] One of the flowers she described was the rare Titan Arum, a plant that blooms infrequently.[24] Painted clumsily in liverish browns, the work reflects her nauseous reaction:

> *It is dark brown and velvety in appearance, and has a thick, fleshy substance under the actual flower, which seems to be in a state of putrefaction. It has a terrible smell—sufficient to poison a whole regiment* [25]

23 'The Romance of Flowers: The Beauty of New Guinea', *Herald,* 1 December 1916.

24 In April 2002, one of the large Titan Arums flowered at the Royal Botanic Gardens in Kew, attracting large crowds and much publicity. See www.kew.org/titan/images.html.

25 *Herald,* 1 December 1916, op. cit.

The following year in 1917, Rowan returned to New Guinea, this time in an attempt to paint every single bird of paradise, of which 52 were already known. She stayed at the Madang Mission House, on the north coast. The area was dotted with efficient German copra plantations and mission stations, where trade in birds and butterflies was rampant. The resident missionary made arrangements for her to be carried in a hammock by a party of guides draped in loin cloths. In the manner that most dealers in plumes operated at the time, the first six birds were brought to her dead. With no intention of painting dead birds, she encouraged the local headhunters, with bribes of tobacco, to deliver them live and housed in cages:

> *The large ones I tucked under my arm and held in that way while I painted them. Some were fierce and hard to hold ... I covered the heads of others with handkerchiefs or a table napkin to keep them a little quieter while I was painting the body ... Painting the birds and flowers of New Guinea really did mean a mustering up of courage, and searching for the Birds of Paradise led me into all sorts of out-of the-way places*[26]

Living under the most primitive conditions in the tropical heat, inevitably her health broke down and, suffering from malaria and fatigue, she was carried by guides down from the high country to the coast, where she was expected to die. With the courage that had seen her through so many intrepid adventures, she rallied and, on return to Australia with over 300 paintings, she went to Macedon to be nursed by her sister Blanche Ryan.

The collection was shown for the first time in Melbourne at the Fine Art Society's Galleries in November 1918. Rowan exhibited 189 paintings: 172 flowers, 40 birds of paradise, 72 fungi, two pictures of coral, a bat, a squirrel and a fish. The *Sun* critic wrote: 'She went to New Guinea with a keen desire to paint the brilliant birds of paradise from life. Hitherto even such notable naturalists as J. Gould, who made a special study of Australian birds, have been content to sketch ... from dead specimens'.[27]

It was after this exhibition that the idea of her works being collected by the National Library of Australia was first mooted, in an impassioned letter by the Speaker of the House of Representatives Elliot Johnson. He wrote:

26 'Painting Rare Birds', *Argus*, Melbourne, 9 November 1918.
27 *Sun*, 13 March 1918. The fungi are reproduced in C. Barrett, *Australian Wildlife* (Melbourne: Georgian House, 1945).

it would be a national calamity if the collection were to be disposed of outside Australia ... although Australia may not be so prolific as America in millionaires there are yet a few citizens who could, without the slightest embarrassment in their financial resources, expend a few thousand pounds ... in the acquisition of so valuable an addition to its Commonwealth Library. The loss of this collection would be irreparable and would, moreover, be for all time a standing reproach to us as a community.[28]

Despite this plea from a man of influence, no financial supporters came forward.

Soon after, a travelling exhibition was arranged across the United States. Consisting of 376 paintings of American and West Indian flowers and 280 New Guinean and north Queensland birds and flowers, the show toured to Stanford University, California, and then via several other venues on to the American Museum of Natural History. Her New Guinean flowers bled off the page in such bold colour and profusion and eroticism as might have made the American modernist Georgia O'Keeffe proud. Indeed, O'Keeffe was living in New York at the time of the show and began painting her own erotic flowers from this point on.

She next turned her attention to painting a series of butterflies from the famous Dodd collection.[29] F.P. Dodd had collected a vast number of rare, tropical butterflies and insects, which he traded to wealthy patrons. These intricate paintings of tropical butterflies and insects, copied from the artistically arranged cases of Dodd, are among Rowan's greatest achievements. Arranged in serried ranks by the professional lepidopterist himself, in a *trompe l'oeil* effect, Rowan has captured the essence of each insect as if caught in nature.[30]

In March 1920, Ellis Rowan made what would be a final gesture to the Australian public when she staged the largest solo exhibition yet held in the country, displaying 1,000 paintings, including her butterflies, at Anthony Hordern's Gallery in Sydney. Except for her birds of paradise, all works were for sale, ranging from 10 to 125 guineas. The sales of the exhibition amounted to over £2,000, making a record for a woman artist at the time.[31]

28 *Argus*, Melbourne, 23 January 1919.

29 Judith McKay suggests that Rowan visited Kuranda in 1911 and probably first saw the Dodd collection at that time; see McKay, op. cit., p. 27. For an account of the Dodd collection, see Geoff Monteith, *The Butterfly Man from Kuranda, Frederick Parkhurst Dodd* (Brisbane: Queensland Museum, 1991).

31 William Moore, *The Story of Australian Art*, Vol. 2, Sydney: Angus and Robertson, 1934, p. 33.

With the future of her life's work still unresolved, Ellis Rowan died at Macedon on 4 October 1922. Her death certificate declared 'heart failure, pulmonary congestion/pleurisy'. Tributes from around Australia poured in to the press: 'To those fortunate to meet her, the painter was more wonderful than her work—and that is saying a great deal. The first impression was of a fiery, intense vitality in a seemingly most fragile personality. Her conversation was brilliant, full of crisp descriptions of people and places ... She had a power of endurance, which strong men might envy ... and worked as if upheld by some power greater than any inherent in human flesh and blood'.[32]

The year after her death, the Commonwealth Government finally purchased 947 of her watercolours for £5,000, thought to be a meagre sum for her sister Blanche, who was the sole survivor and executrix. These works have been housed since then in the collections of the National Library of Australia.

Patricia Fullerton
Writer and curator

This is an abridged version of an essay originally published in The Flower Hunter: Ellis Rowan *(Canberra: NLA Publishing, 2002).*

32 Winifred Scott, 'An Appreciation', *Ellis Rowan's Newspaper Cuttings Book 1895–1922*, Manuscripts Collection, National Library of Australia (MS2203).

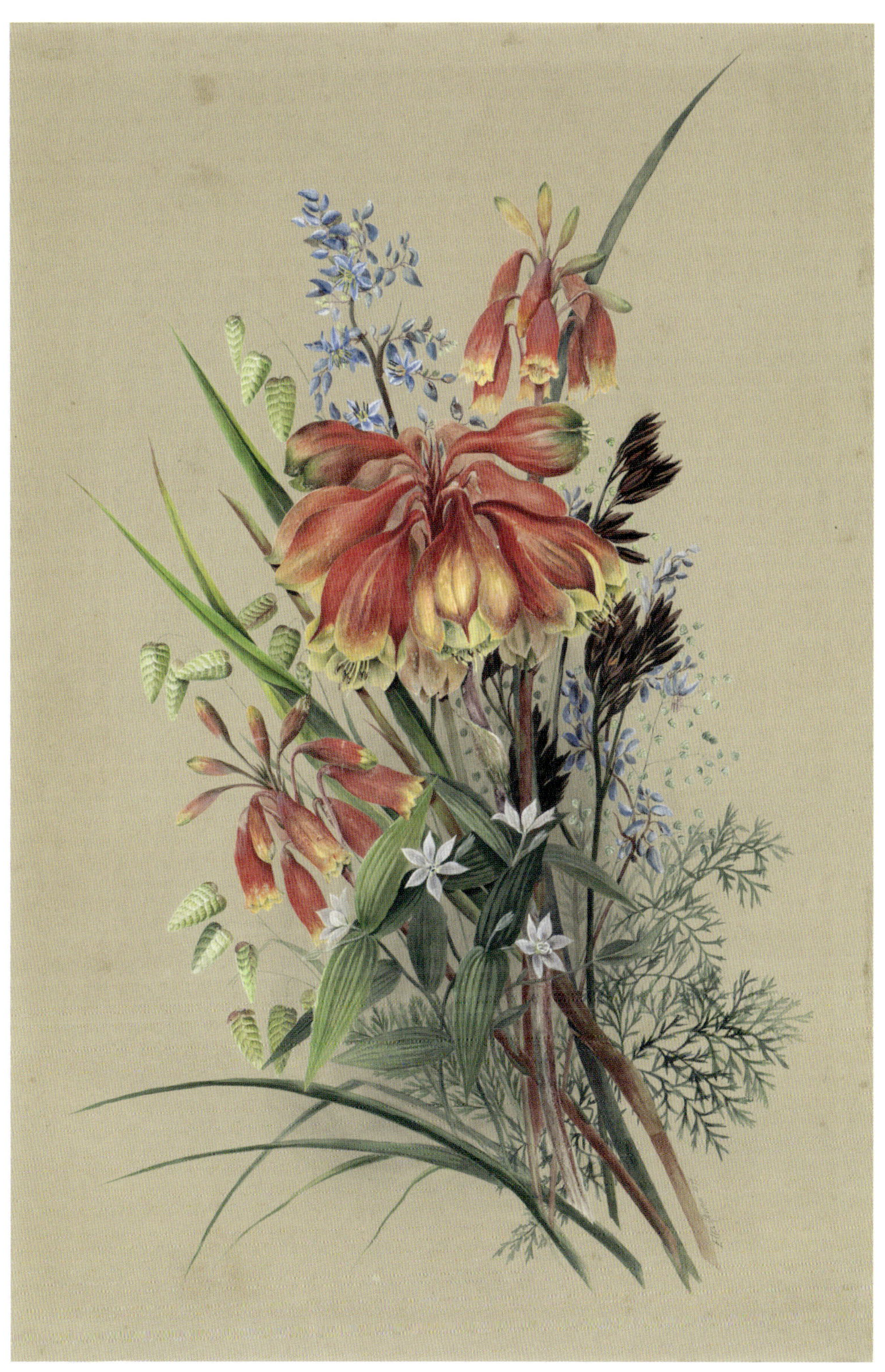

Christmas Bells, Flax Lily, Bloodroot and Grasses 1879
gouache and watercolour on paper; 53.7 x 37.2 cm; Western Australia
nla.cat-vn1322031

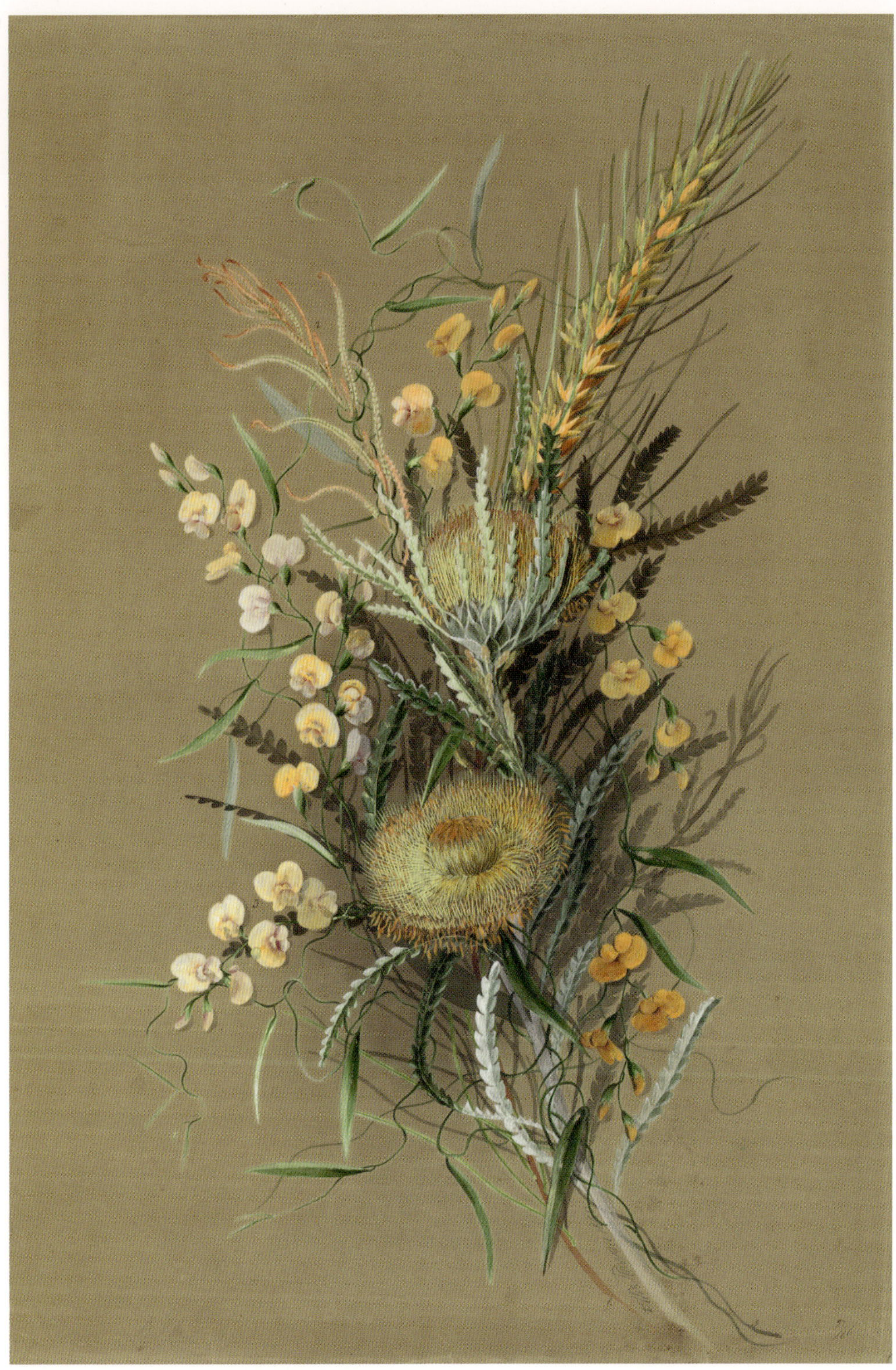

Geebung, Showy Dryandra and Flame Pea 1880
gouache and watercolour on paper; 54.4 x 37.9 cm; Albany, Western Australia
nla.cat-vn2859875

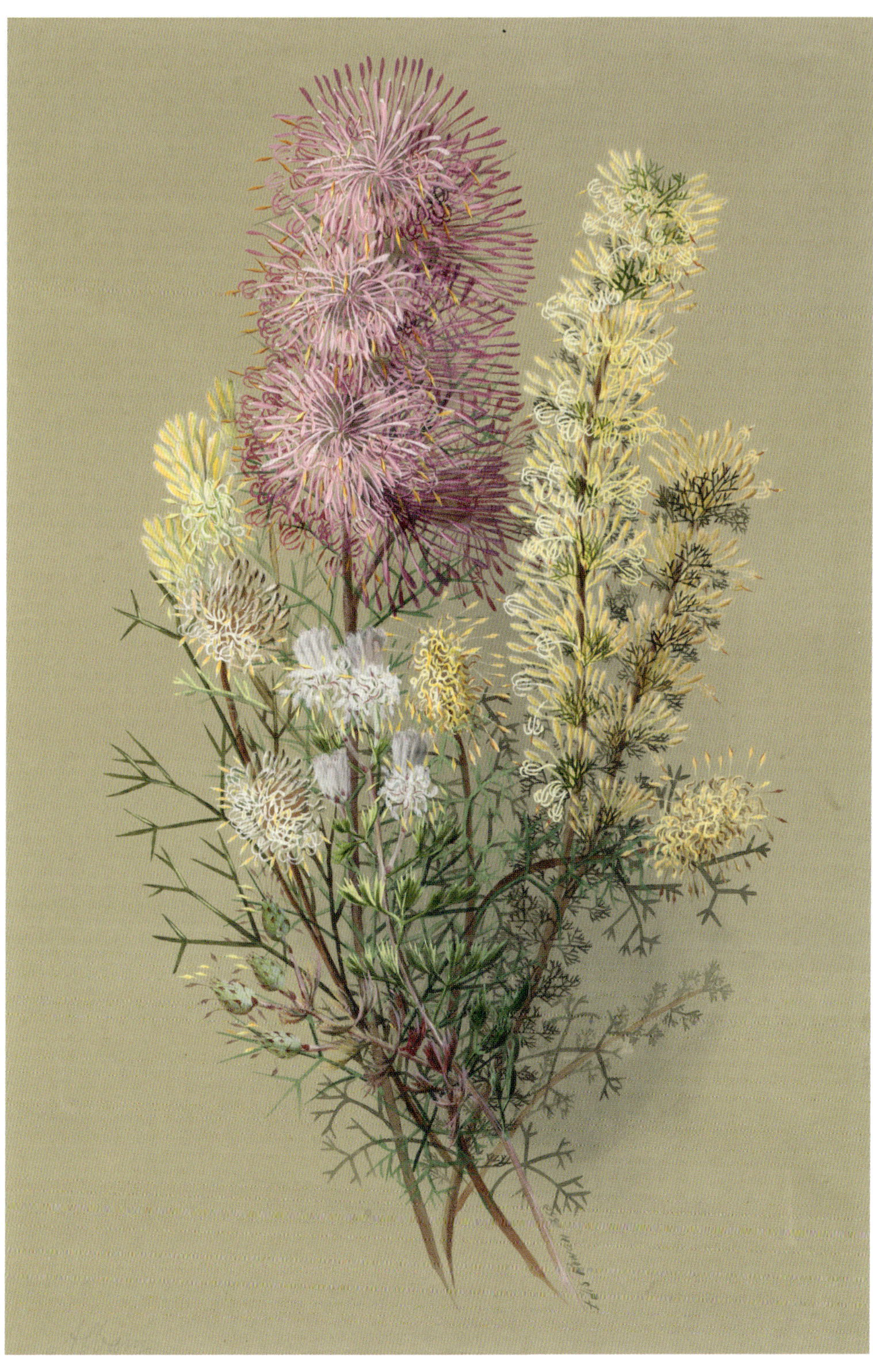

Rose Coneflower, Conebush, Pixie Mops and Nodding Coneflower 1880
gouache and watercolour on paper; 54.5 x 38 cm; Albany, Western Australia
nla.cat-vn2859809

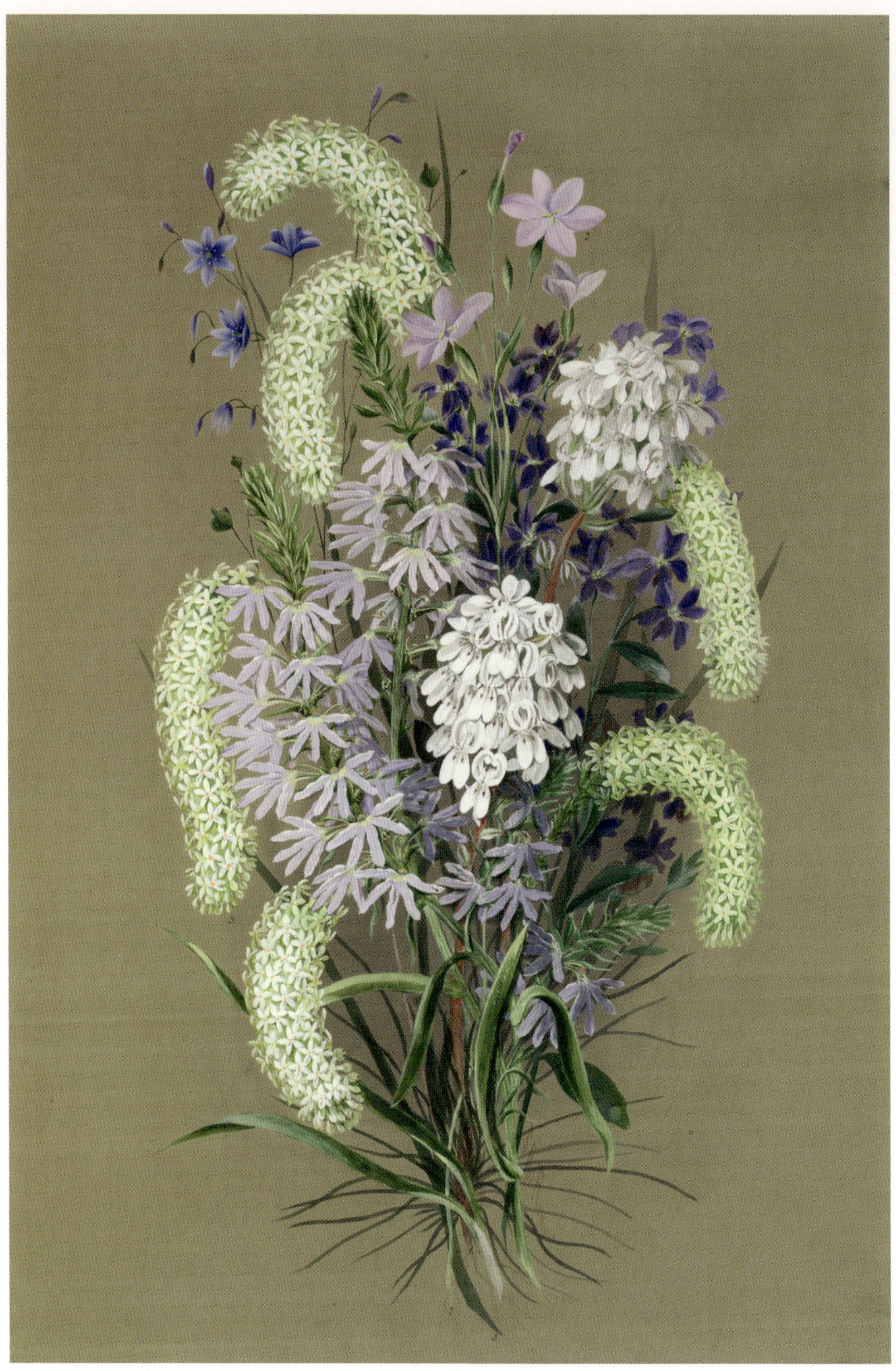

Posy Triggerplant, Morning Iris, Fan Flower, Candles and Blue Stars 1880
gouache and watercolour on paper; 54.5 x 38 cm; Champion Bay, Western Australia
nla.cat-vn1335096

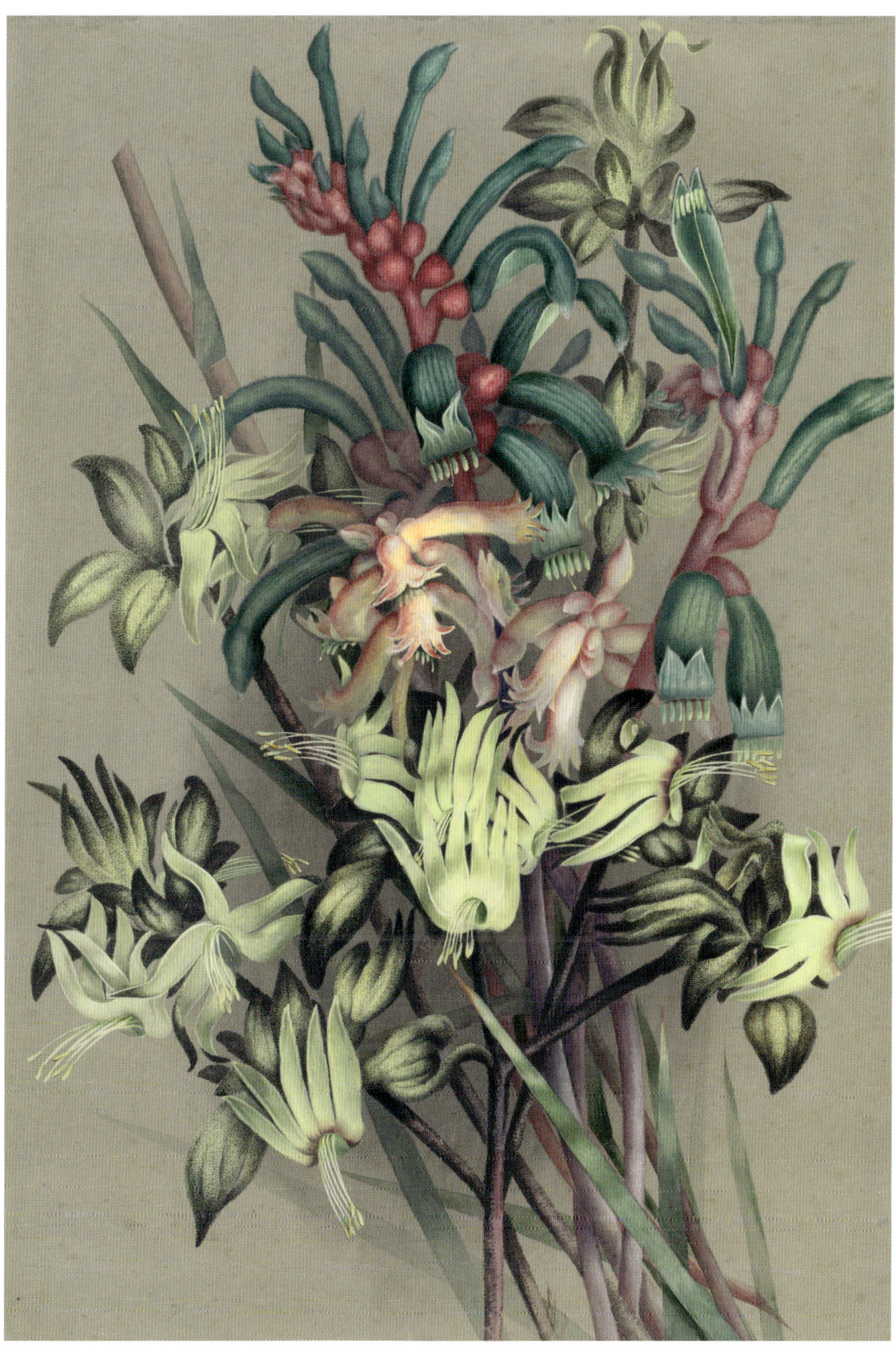

Black Kangaroo Paw, Mangles' Kangaroo Paw and Catspaw c.1880
gouache and watercolour on paper; 54.7 x 38 cm; Perth, Western Australia
nla.cat-vn2683556

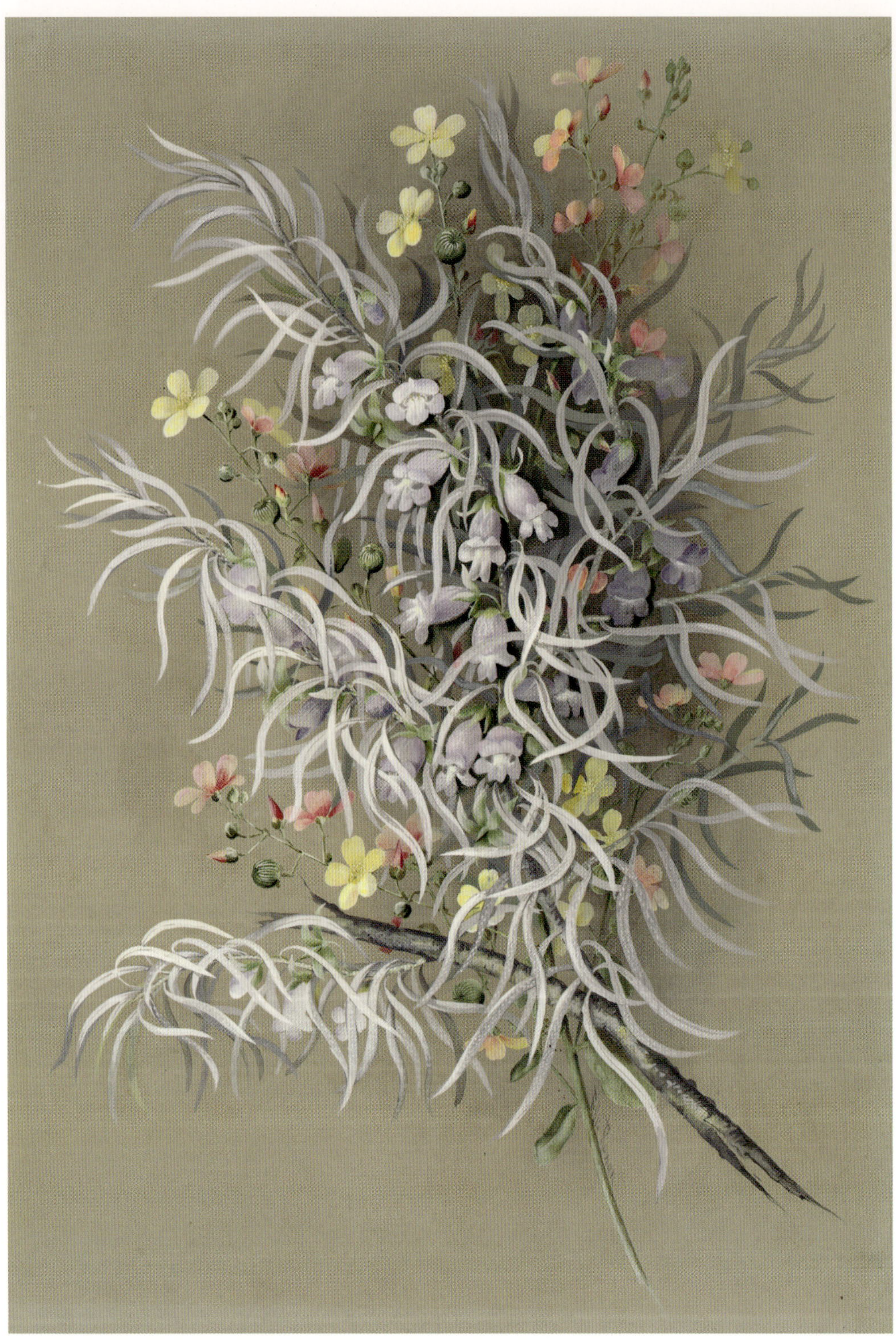

Indian Mallow and Emu Bush c.1880
gouache and watercolour on paper; 54.7 x 37.8 cm; Carnarvon, Western Australia
nla.cat-vn1334979

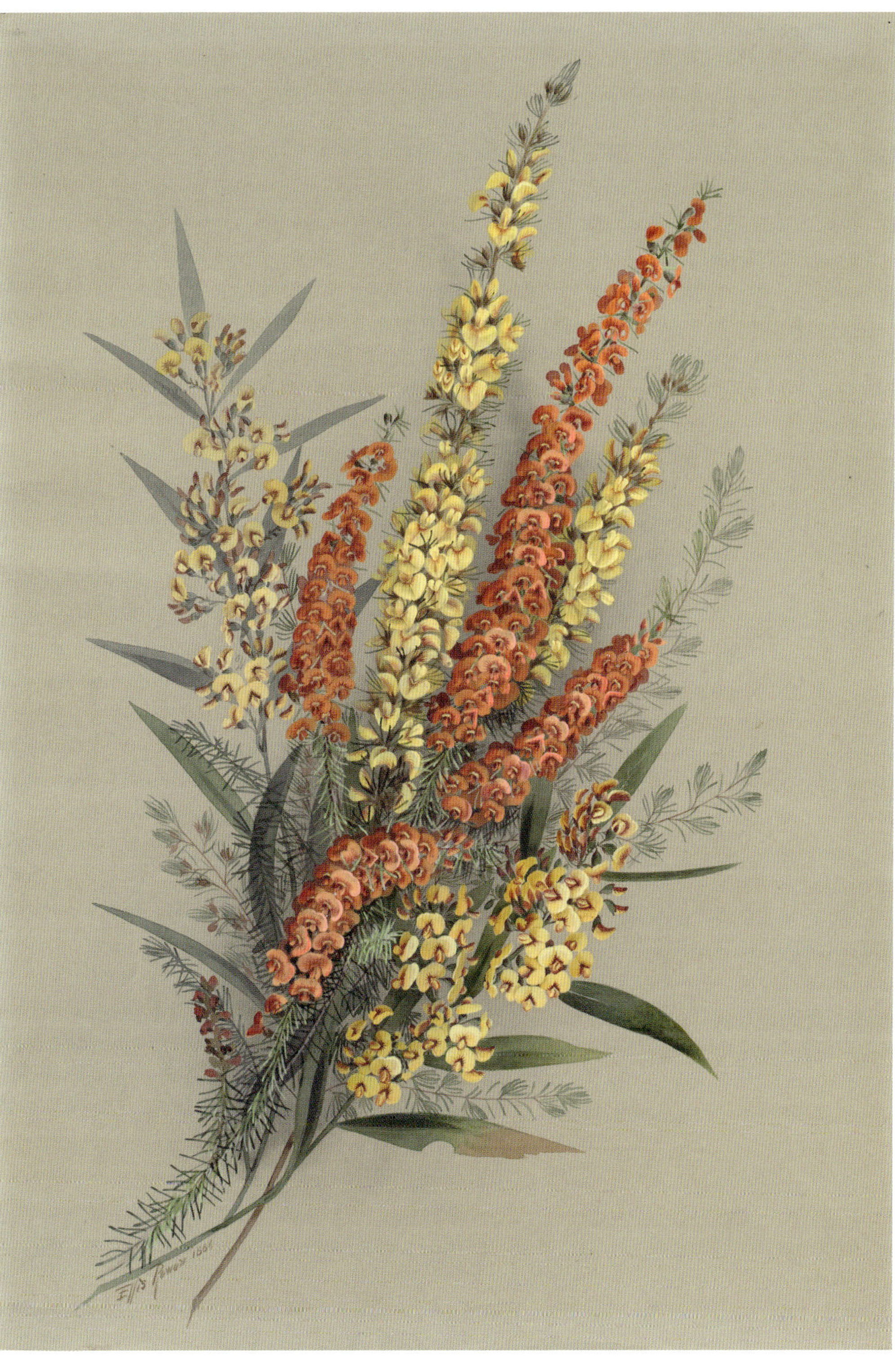

Narrow-leaf Bitter Pea, Guinea Flower Bush Pea and Showy Parrot-pea 1886
gouache and watercolour on paper; 51.8 x 38 cm
nla.cat-vn2688899

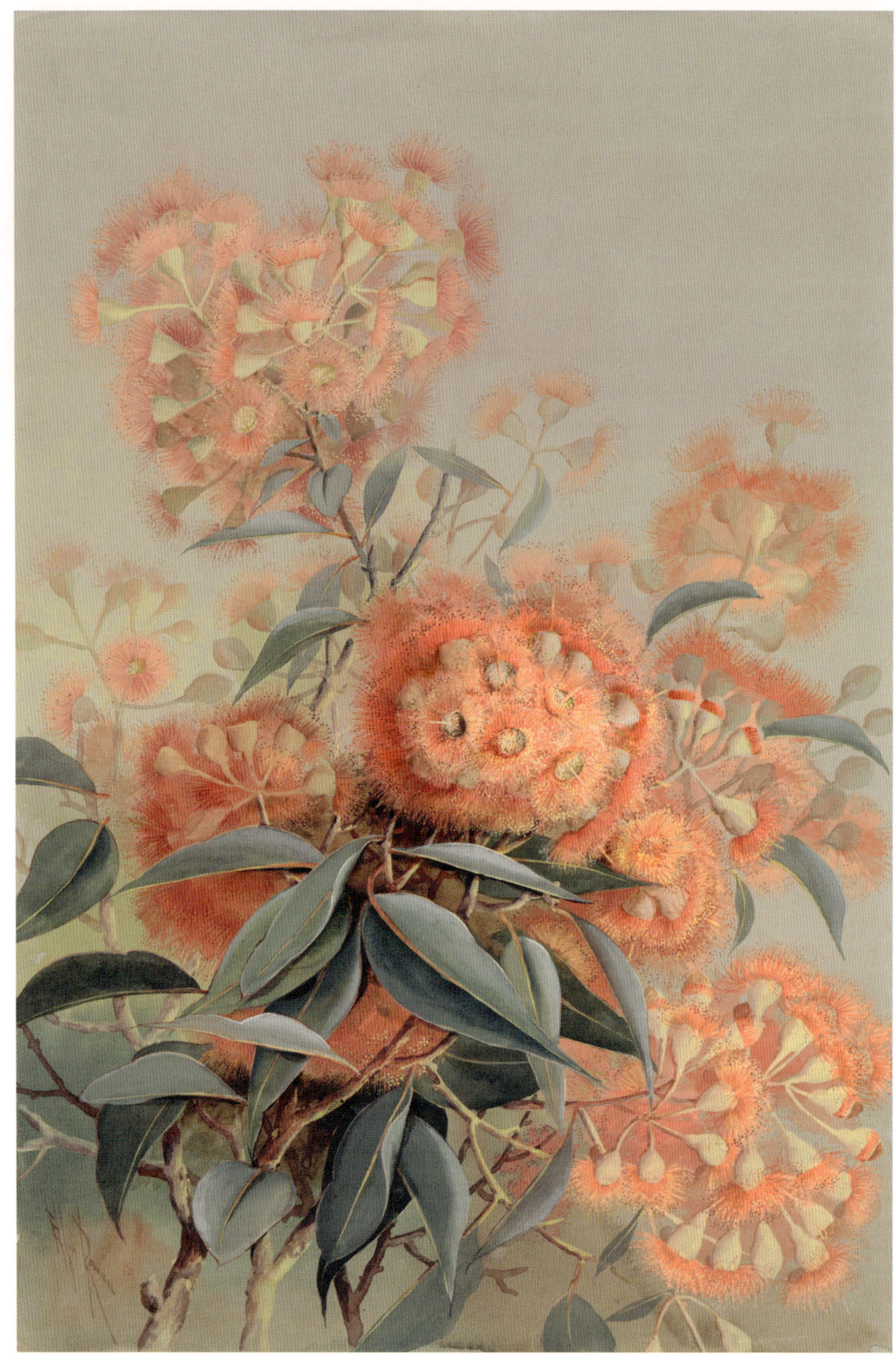

Red-flowering Gum c.1886
gouache and watercolour on paper; 56 x 38 cm; Western Australia
nla.cat-vn1167196

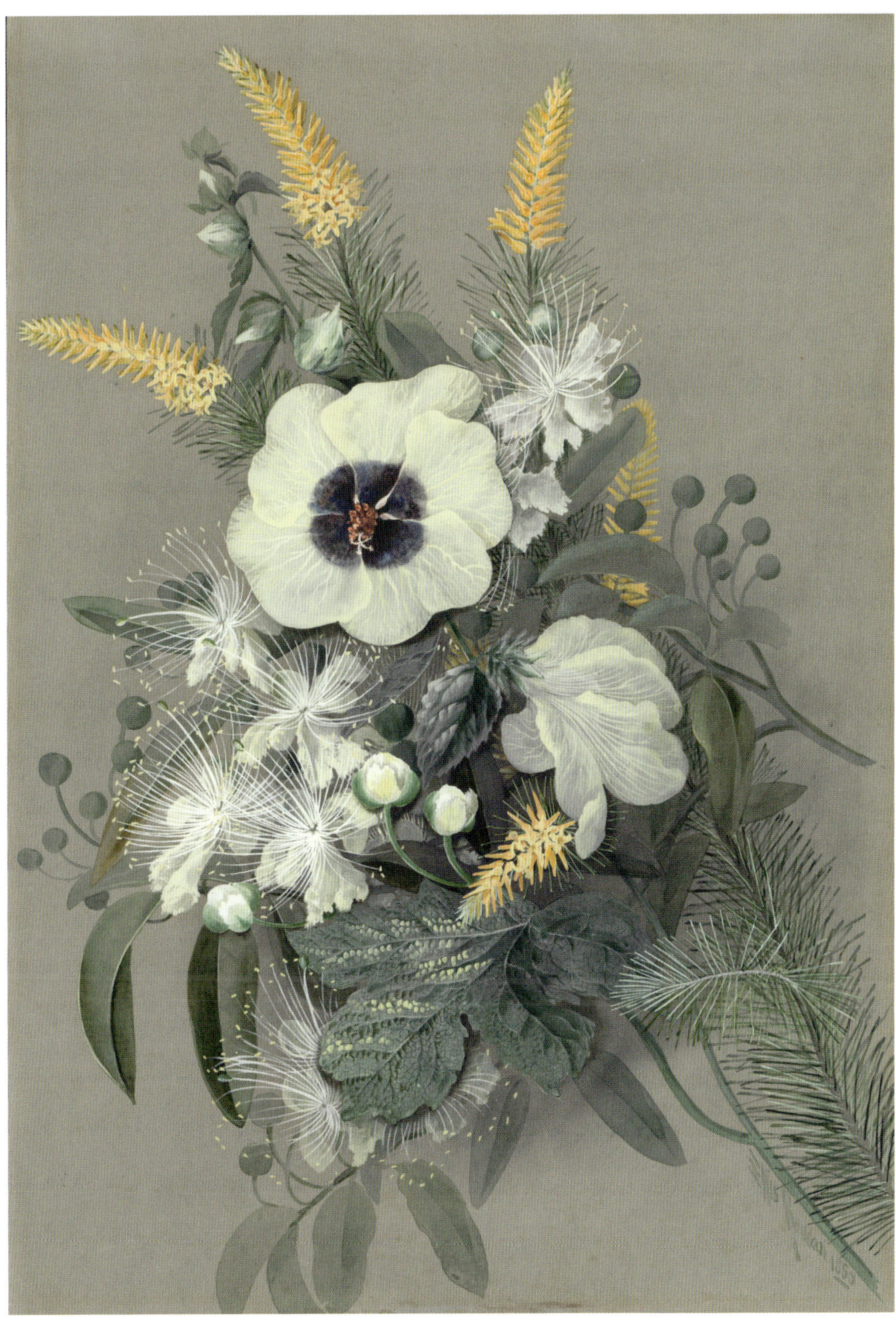

Pine-leaf Geebung, Brush Caper Berry and Rose Mallow 1886
gouache and watercolour on paper; 54.5 x 38 cm; New South Wales
nla.cat-vn2689551

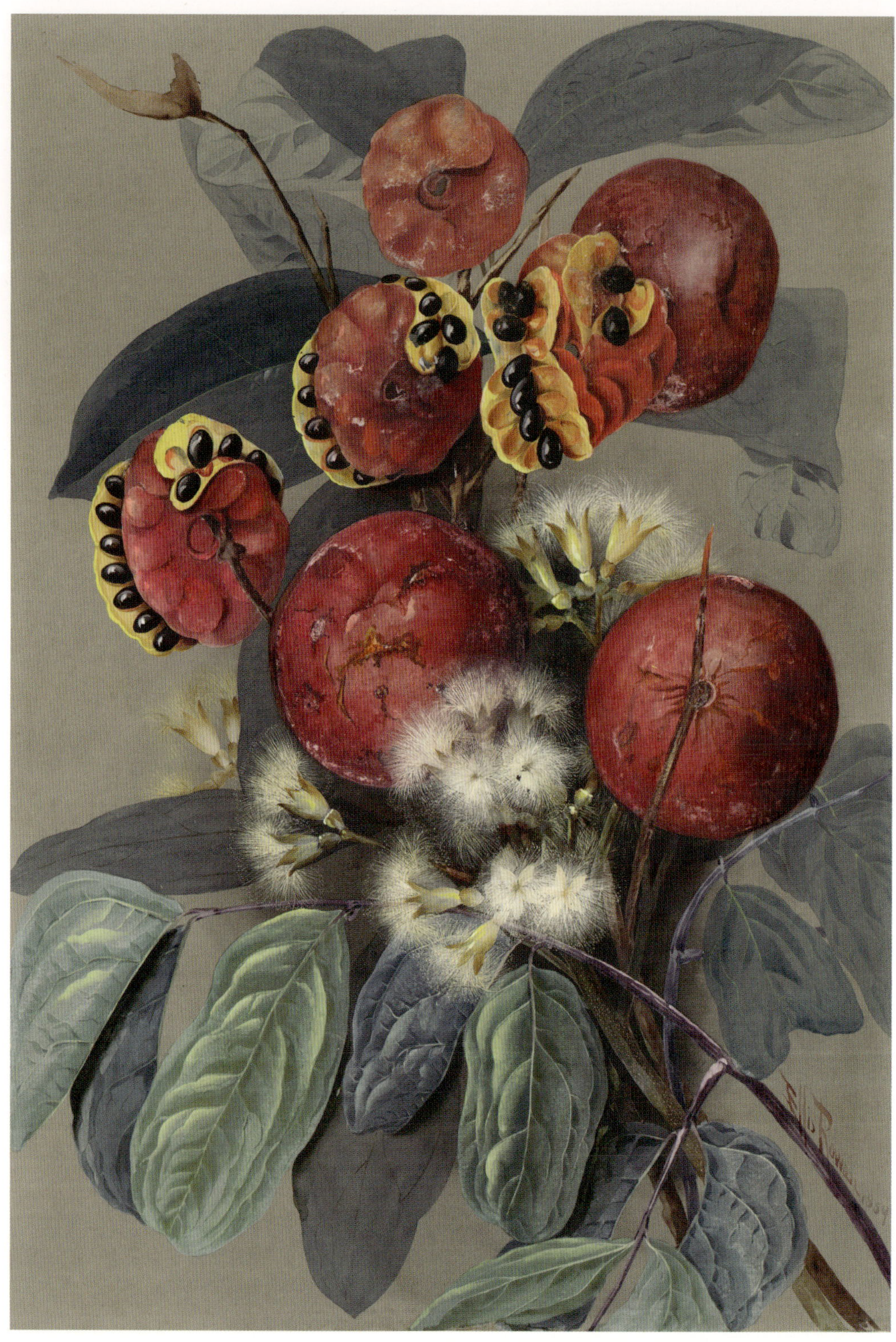

Salmon Bean 1887
gouache and watercolour on paper; 54.8 x 38 cm; Johnstone River, Queensland
nla.cat-vn2843843

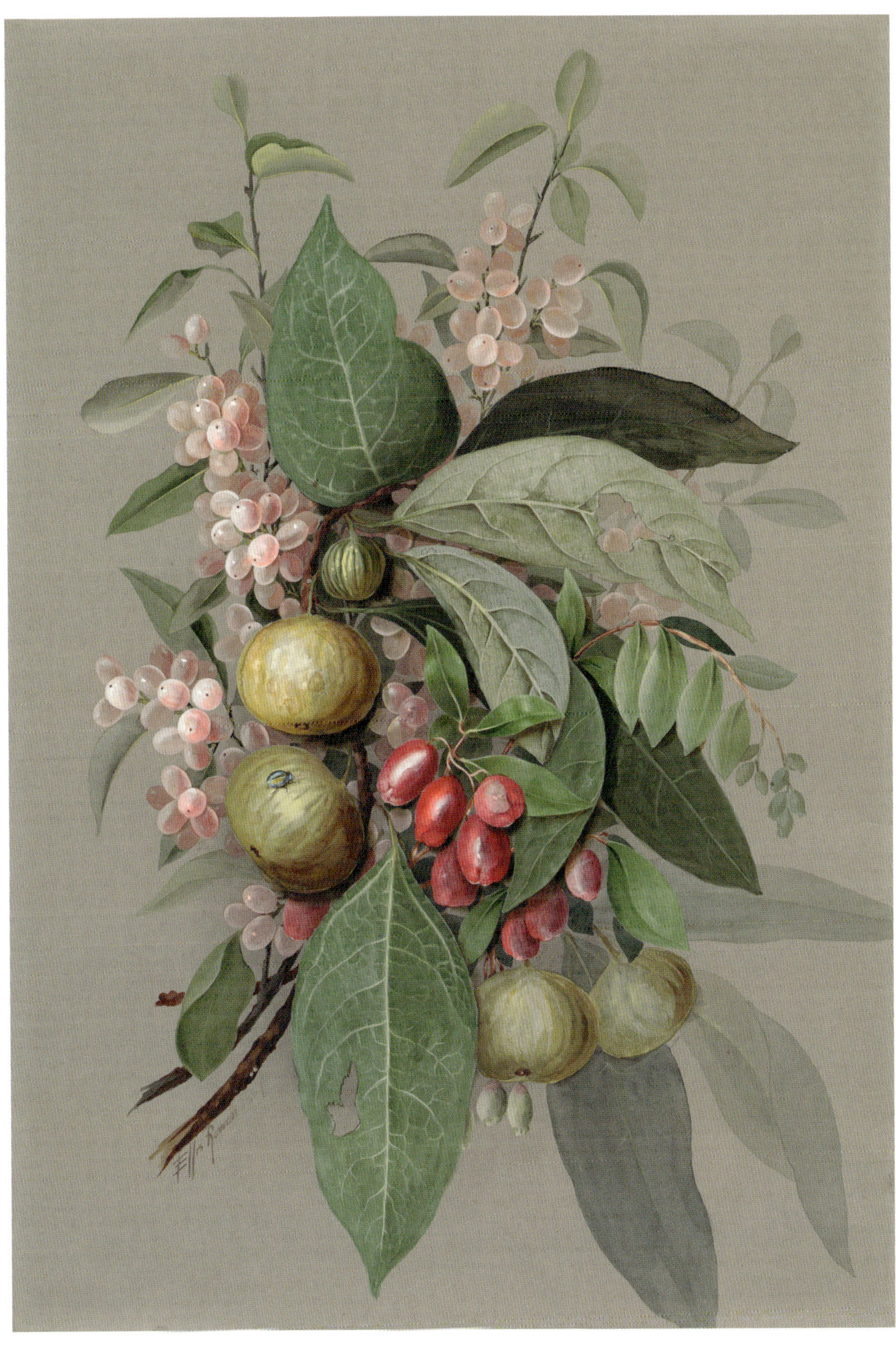

Brush Cherry, Clausena and Black Walnut 1887
gouache and watercolour on paper, 34.7 x 38 cm, Johnstone River, Queensland
nla.cat-vn2859656

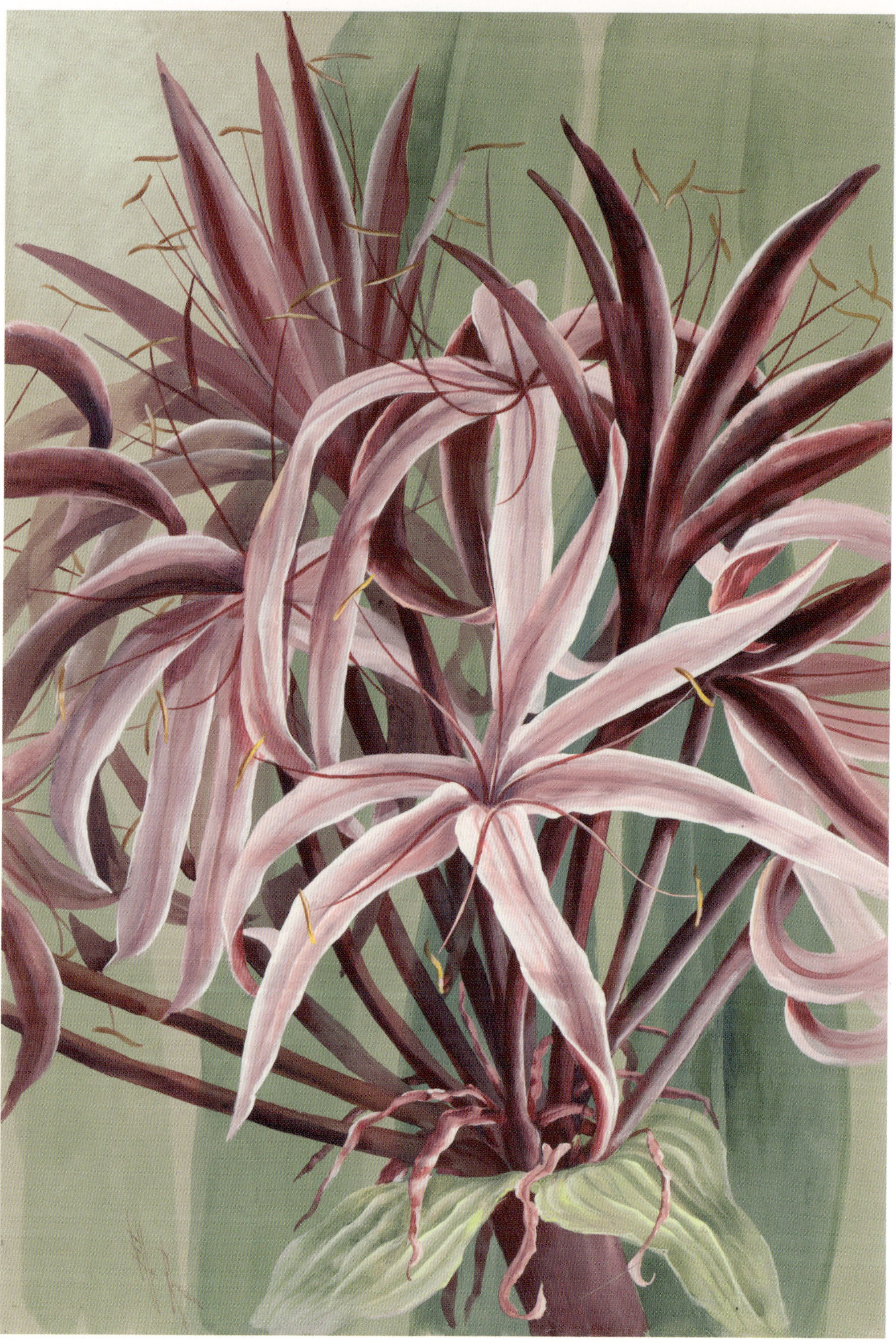

Spider Lily 1887
gouache and watercolour on paper; 54.7 x 37.9 cm; Queensland
nla.cat-vn1316506

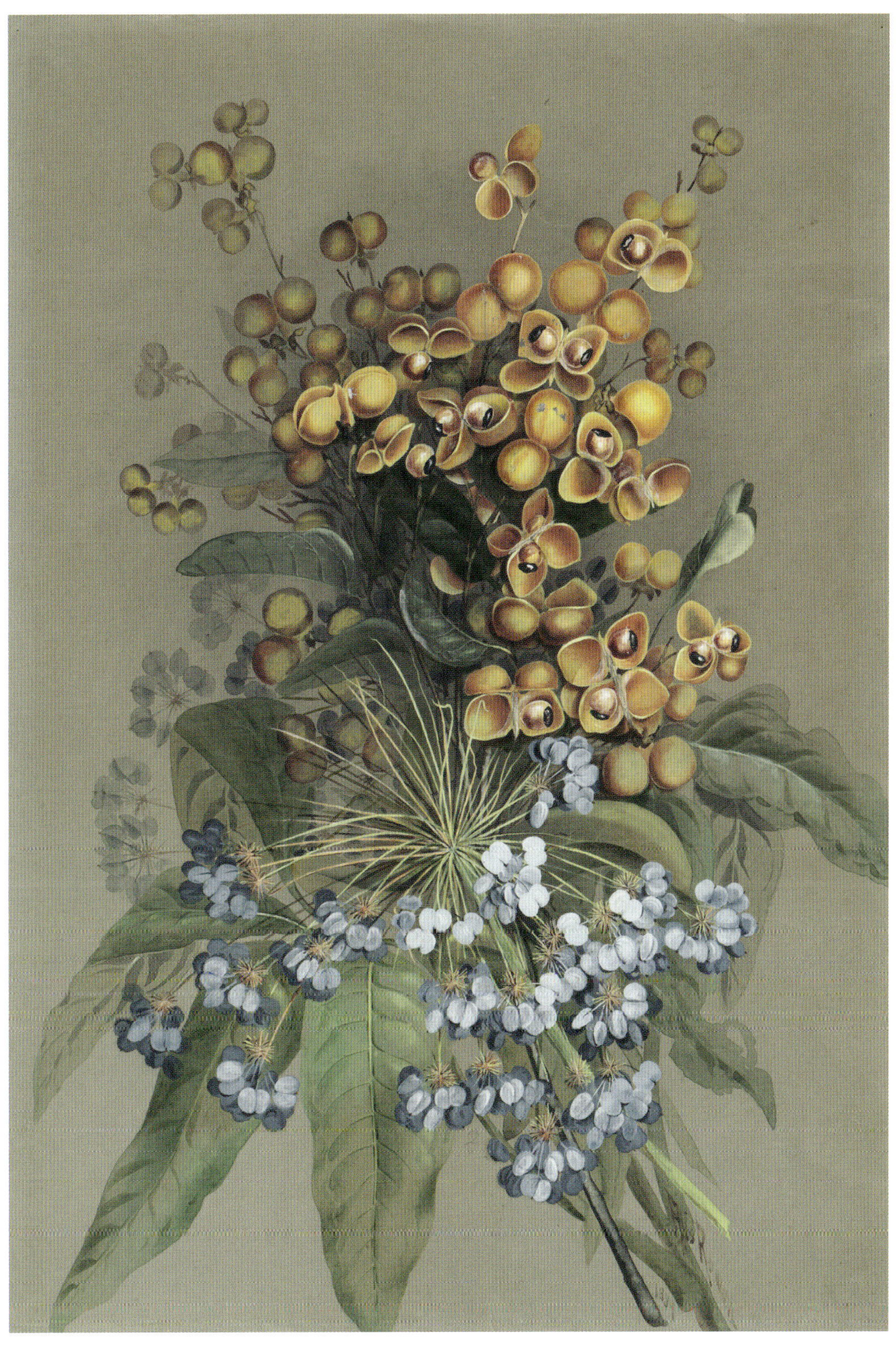

Tulipwood and Blue Umbrella 1887
gouache and watercolour on paper; 54.6 x 38 cm; Mackay, Queensland
nla.cat-vn1317709

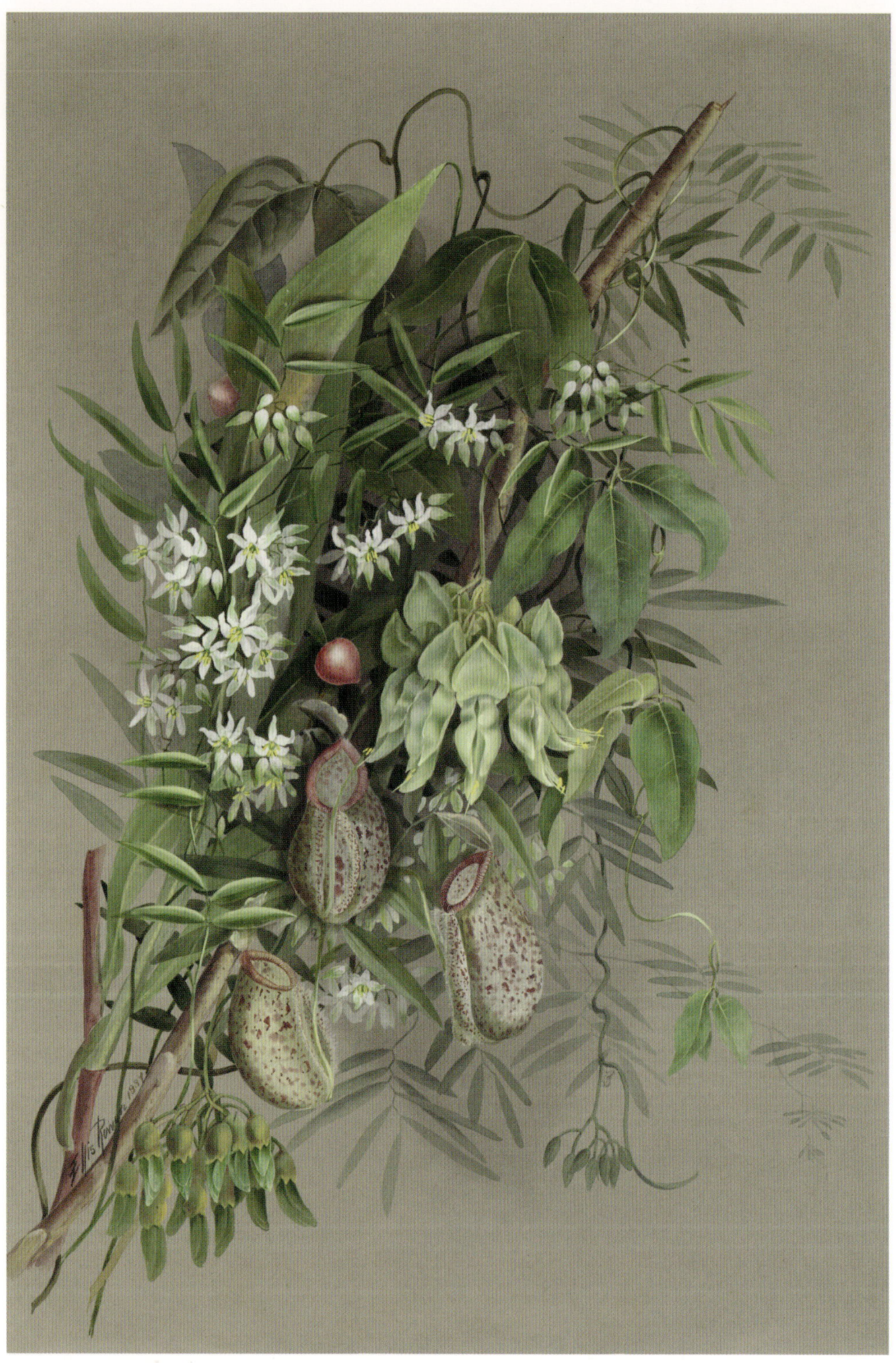

Velvet Bean, Pitcher Plant and Scrambling Lily 1887
gouache and watercolour on paper; 54.5 x 38 cm; Mackay, Queensland
nla.cat-vn1315657

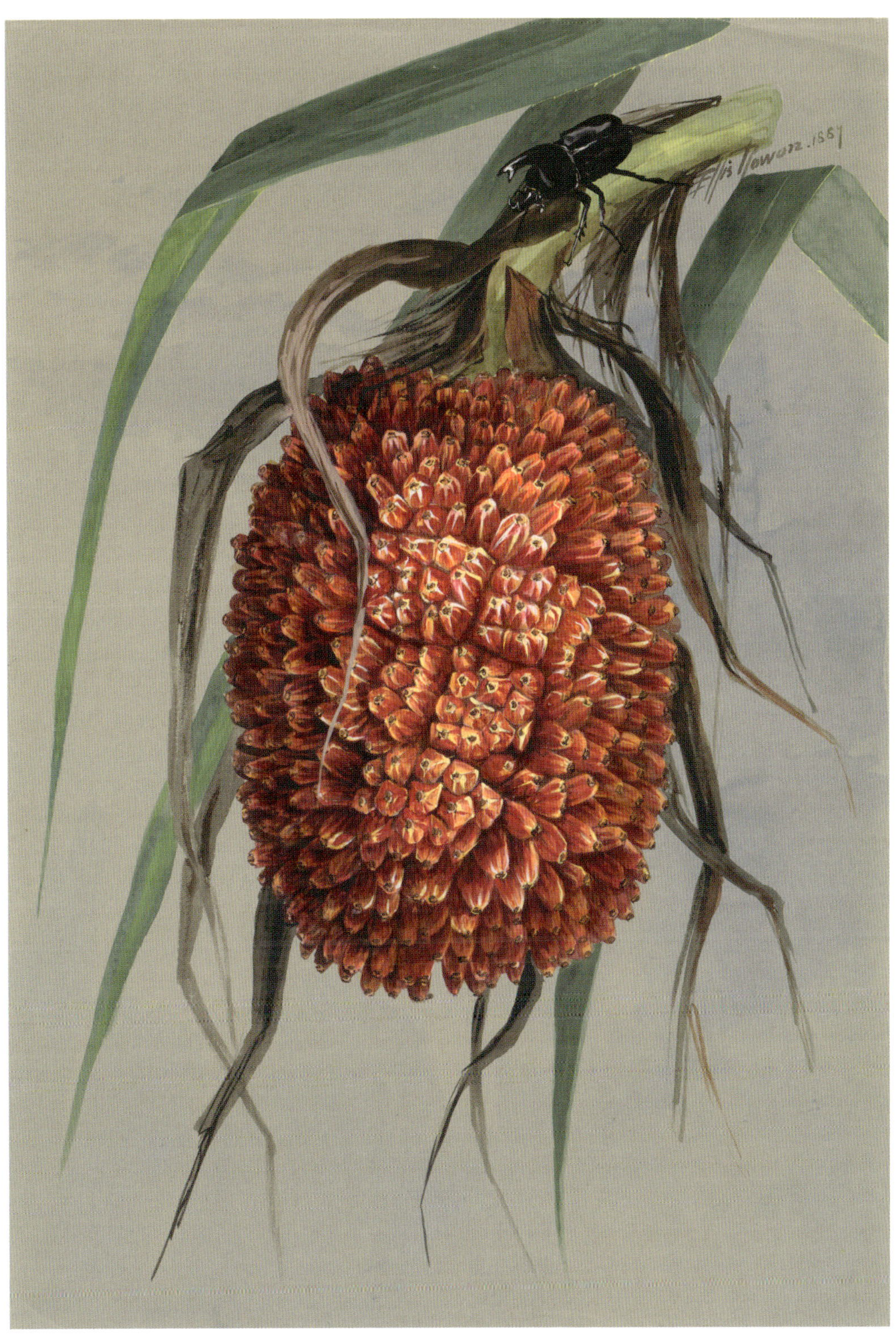

Screw Pine 1887
gouache and watercolour on paper; 54.5 x 38 cm; Mackay, Queensland
nla.cat-vn2689546

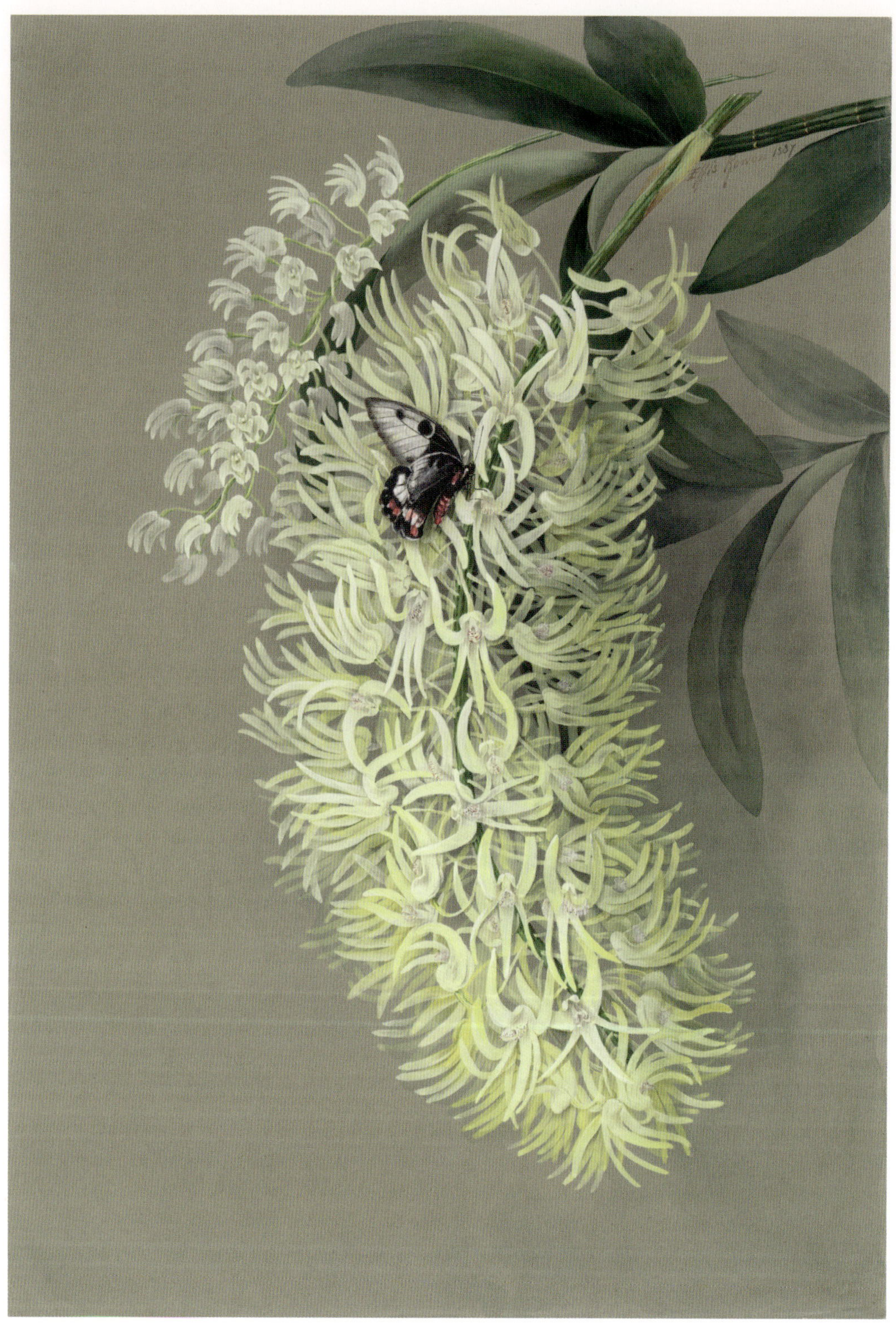

Rock Lily 1887
gouache and watercolour on paper; 54.7 x 38 cm; Queensland
nla.cat-vn1317632

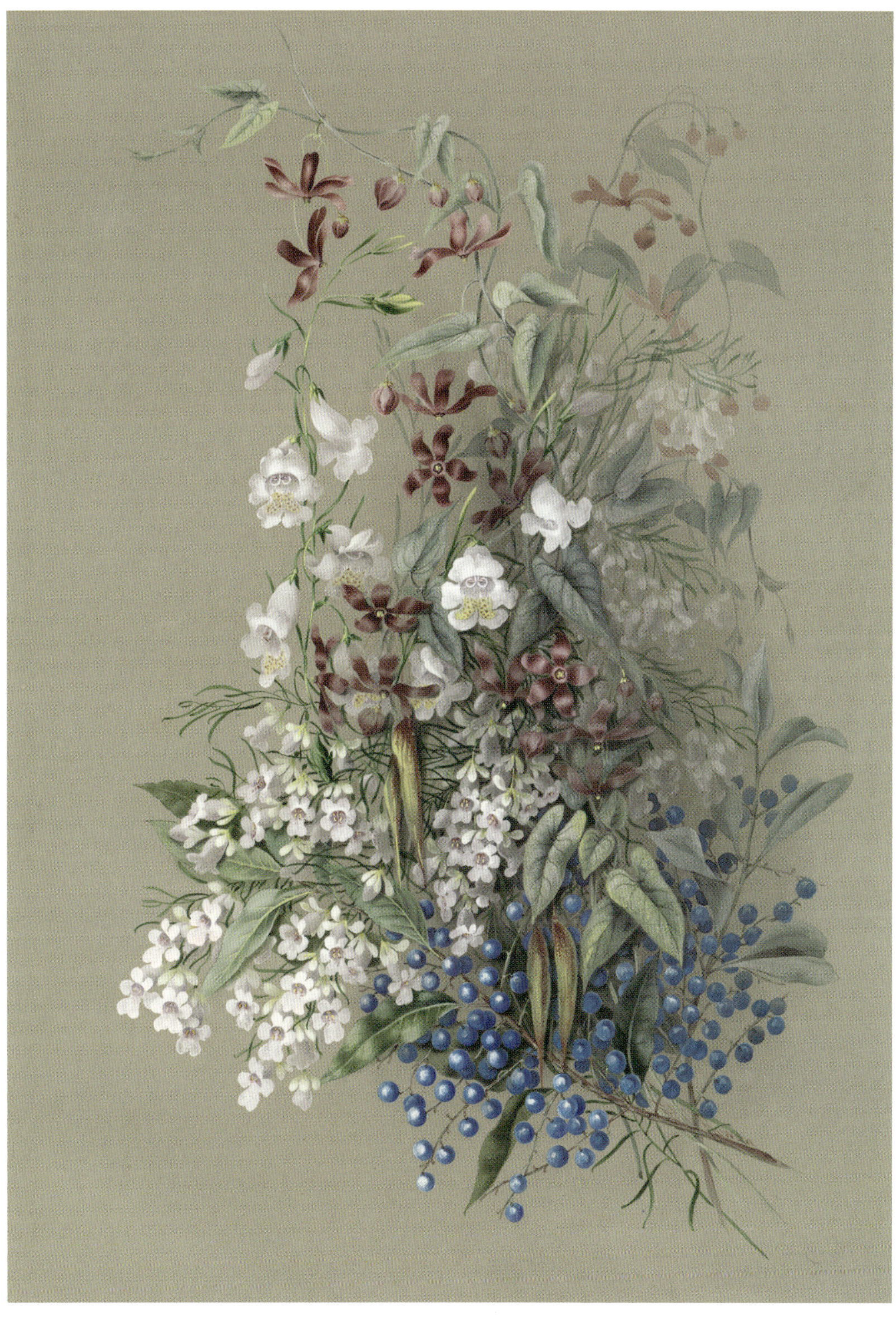

Small-leaved Tylophora, Bignonia, Emu Bush and Blueberry Ash 1887
gouache and watercolour on paper; 54.7 x 38.8 cm; Queensland
nla.cat-vn1316680

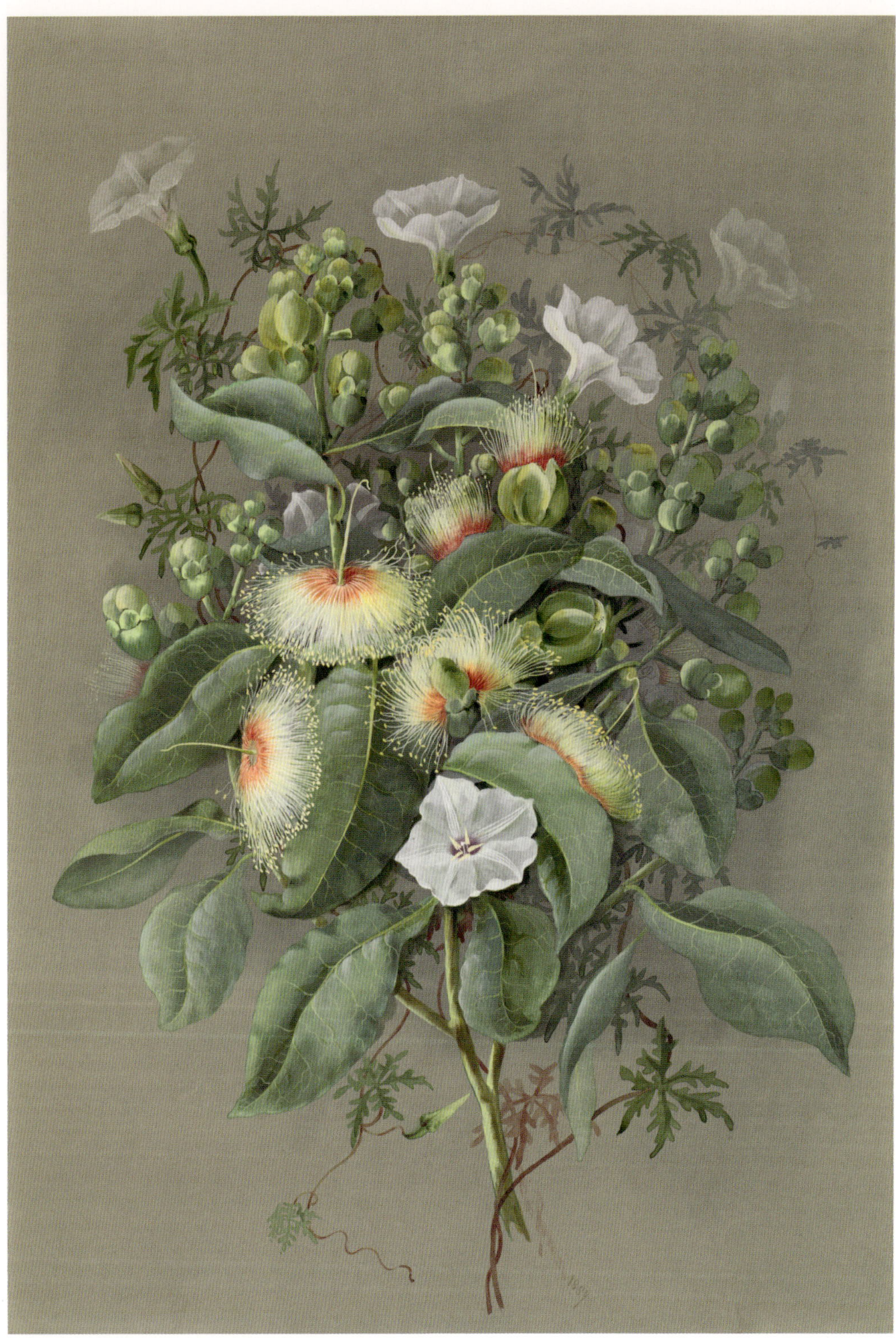

Cocky Apple and Morning Glory c.1887
gouache and watercolour on paper; 54.8 x 38 cm; Dungeness, Herbert River, Queensland
nla.cat-vn2689107

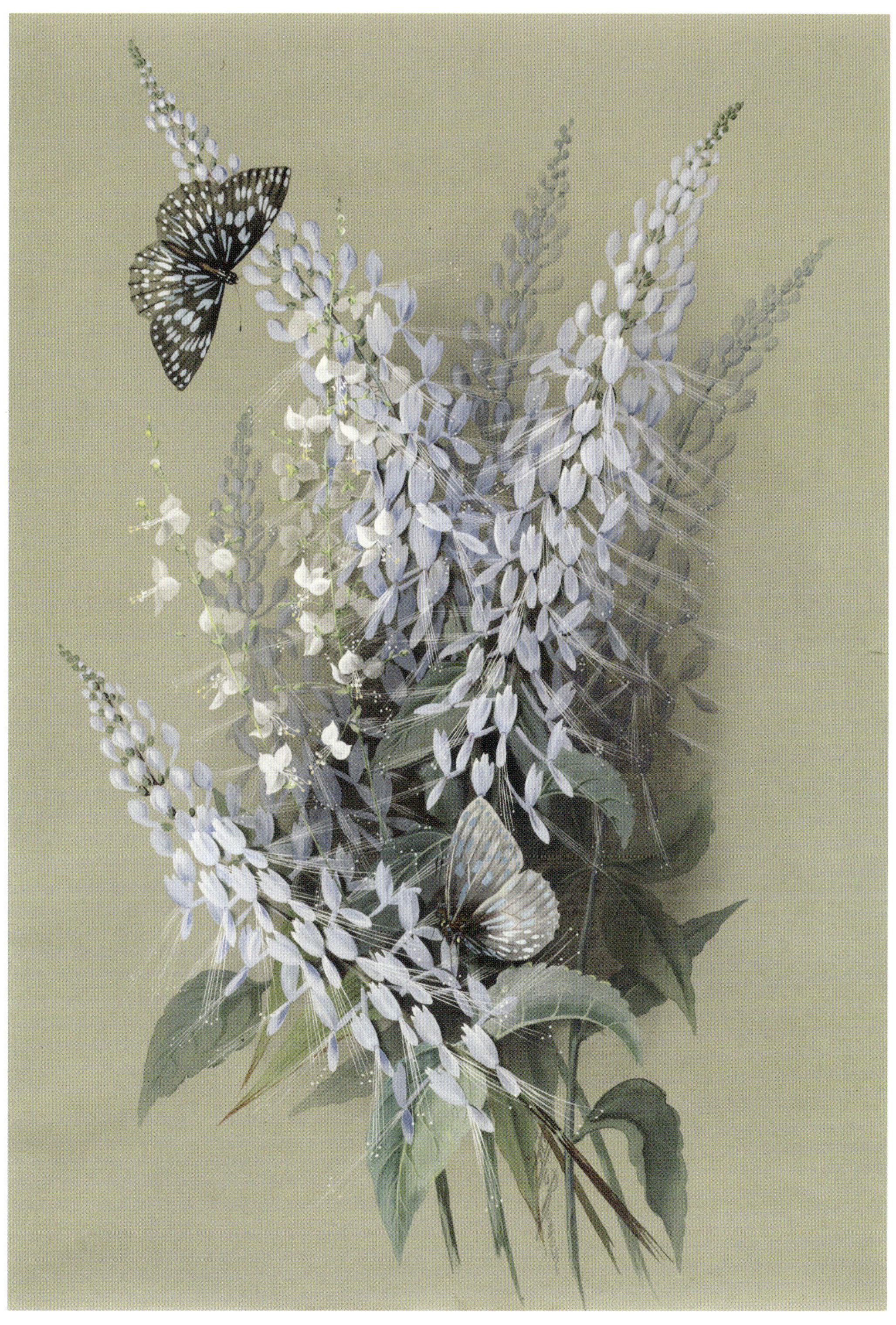

Cats' Whiskers c.1887
gouache and watercolour on paper; 54 x 37.5 cm; Queensland
nla.cat-vn1167210

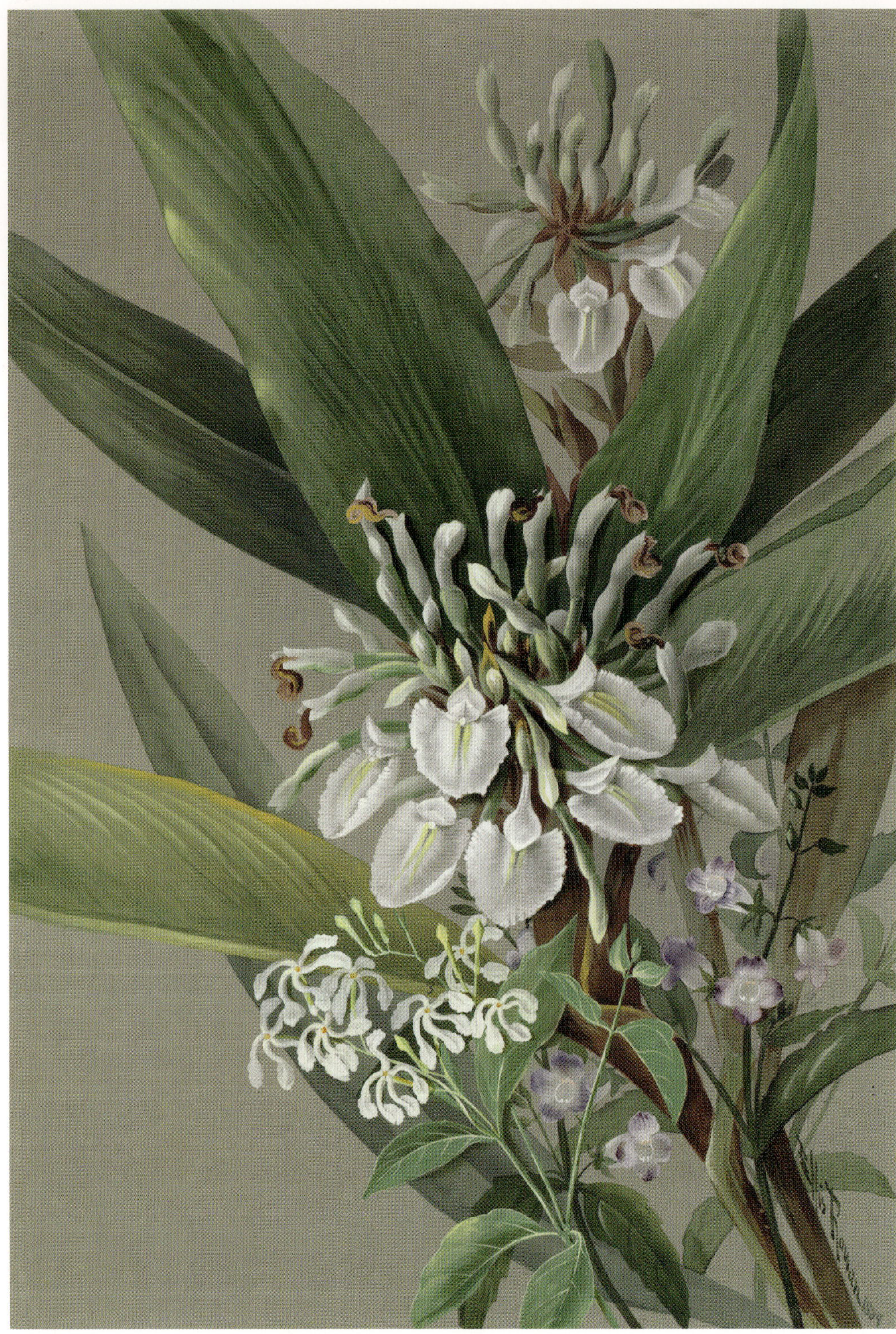

Koala Bells, Eastern Gondola Bush and Native Ginger c.1887
gouache and watercolour on paper; 54.7 x 38 cm; Herbert River, Queensland
nla.cat-vn2848547

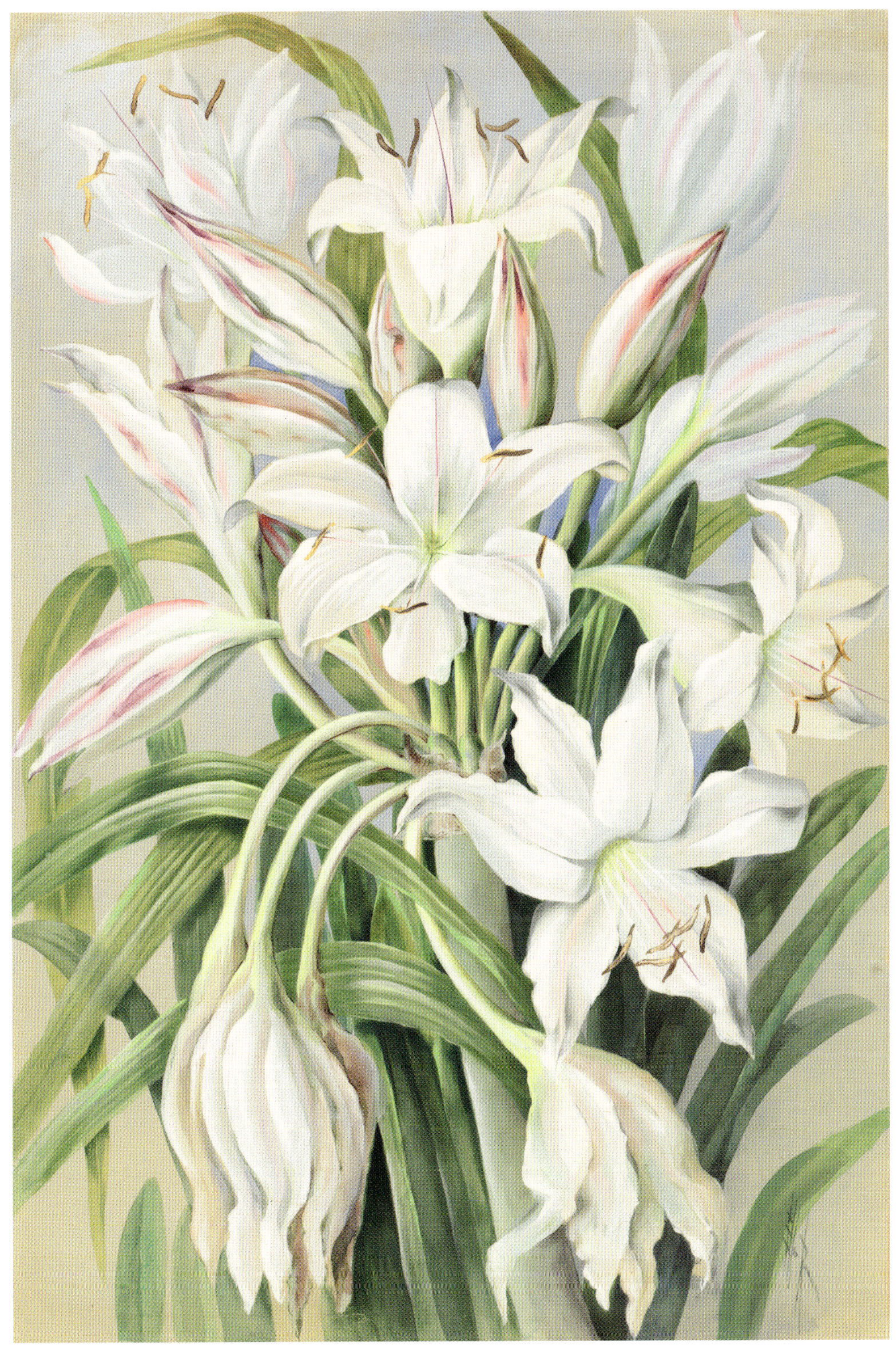

Darling Lily c.1887
gouache and watercolour on paper; 56 x 38 cm; Queensland
nla.cat-vn2683441

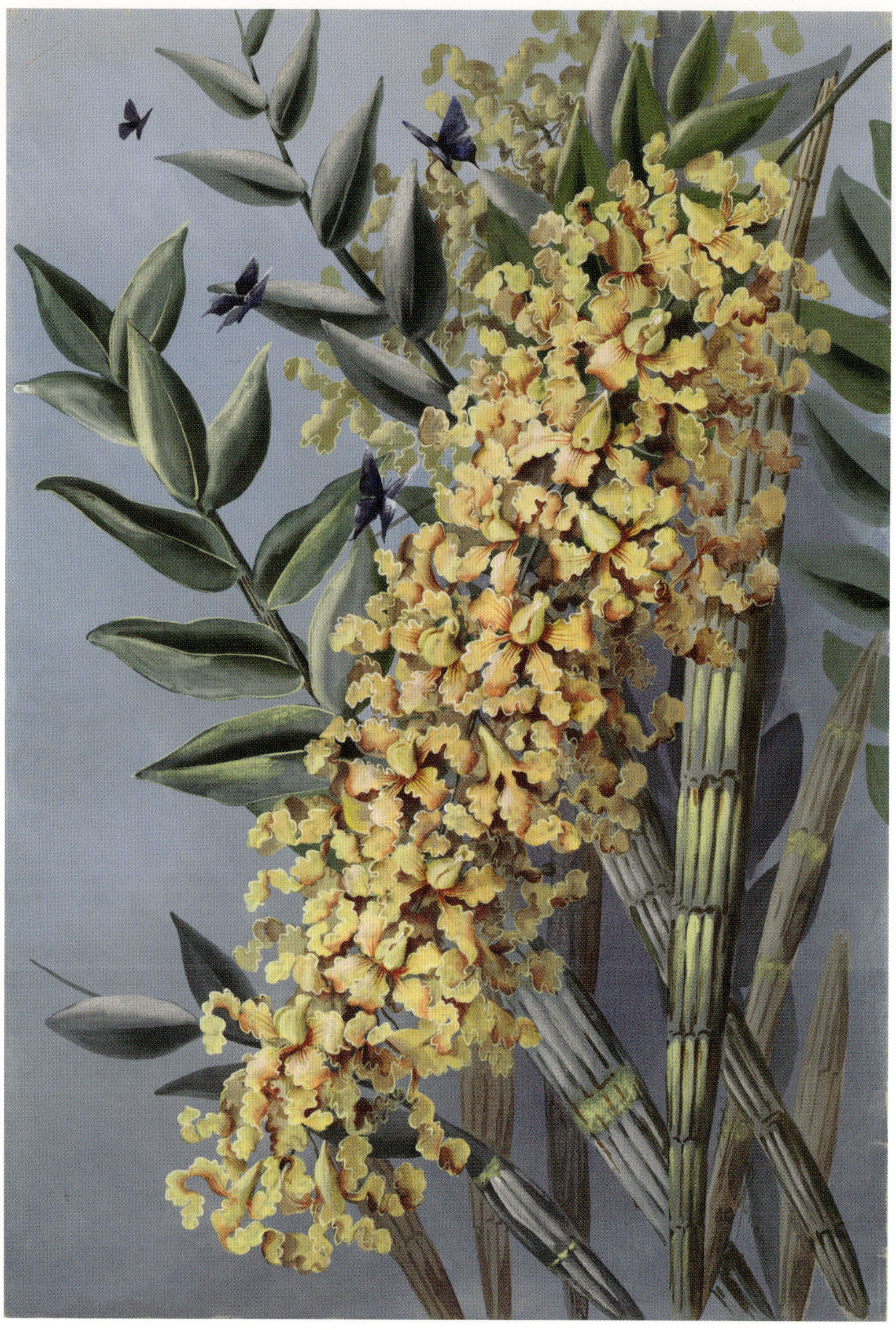

Brown Antler Orchid c.1887
gouache and watercolour on paper; 54.5 x 38 cm; Queensland
nla.cat-vn1326426

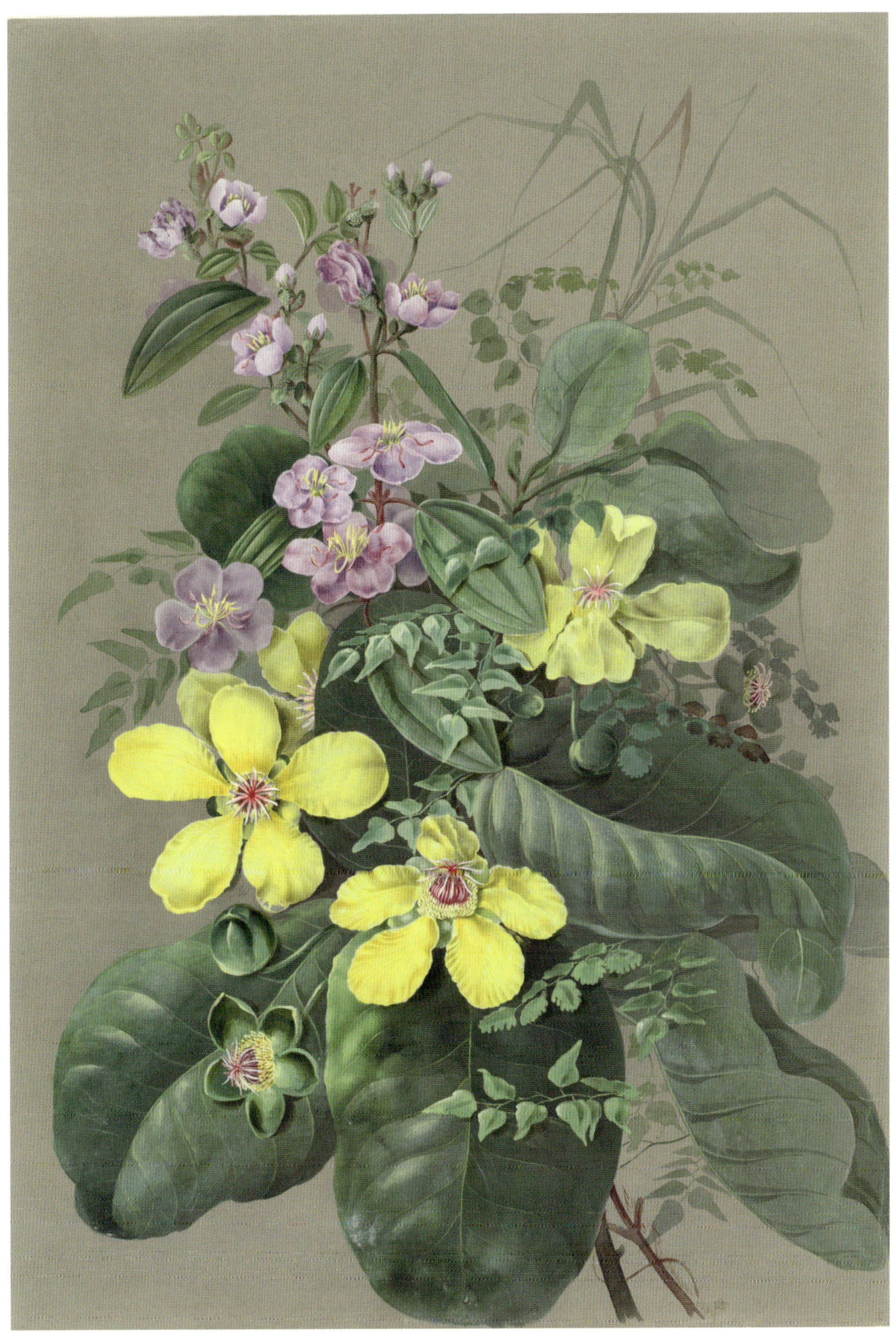

Pink Lasiandra, Golden Guinea Tree and Maidenhair Fern c.1887
gouache and watercolour on paper; 54.8 x 38.2 cm; Herbert River, Queensland
nla.cat-vn1322857

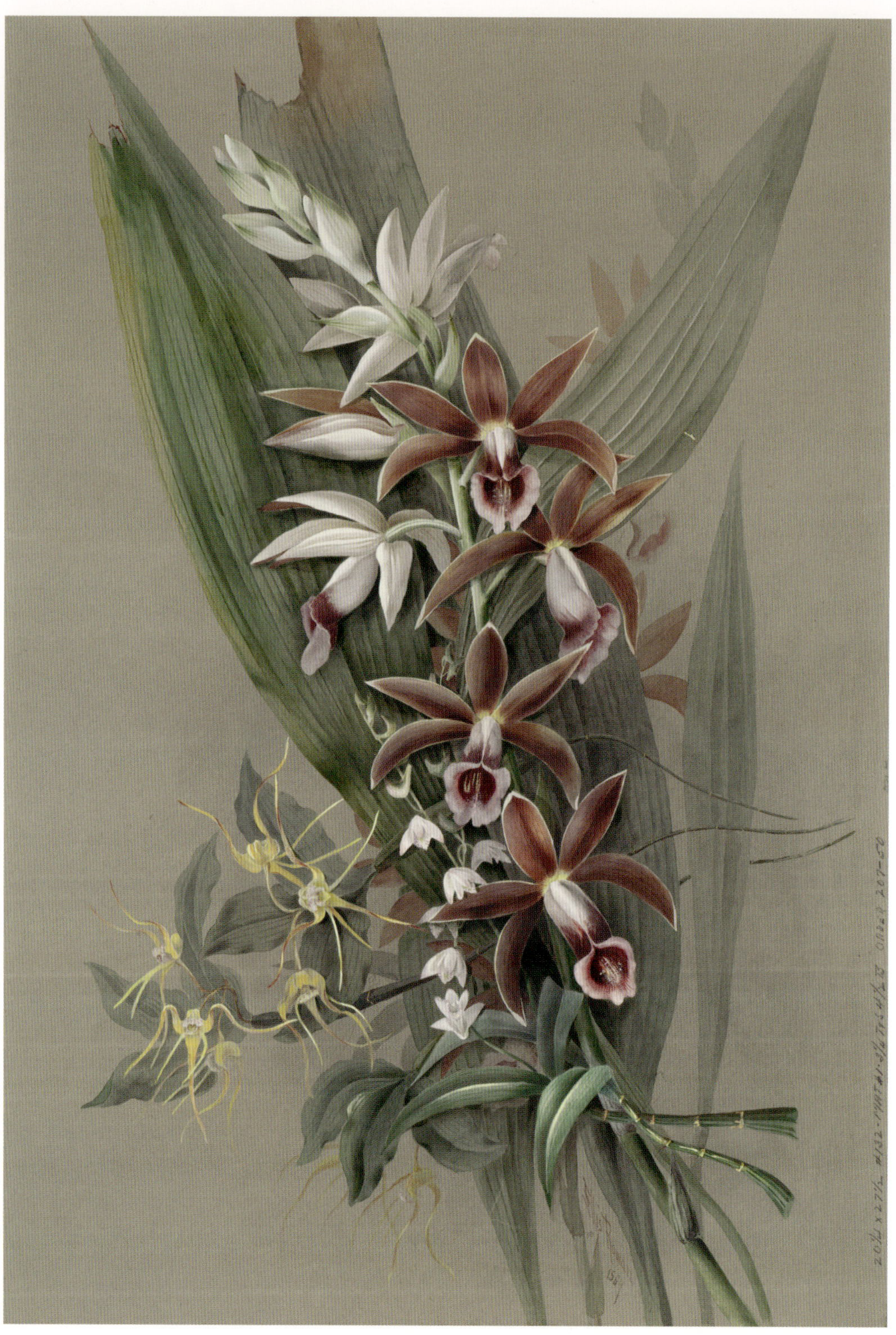

Swamp Orchid and Yellow Tree Spider Orchid c.1887
gouache and watercolour on paper; 54.7 x 38 cm; Mackay, Queensland
nla.cat-vn1326234

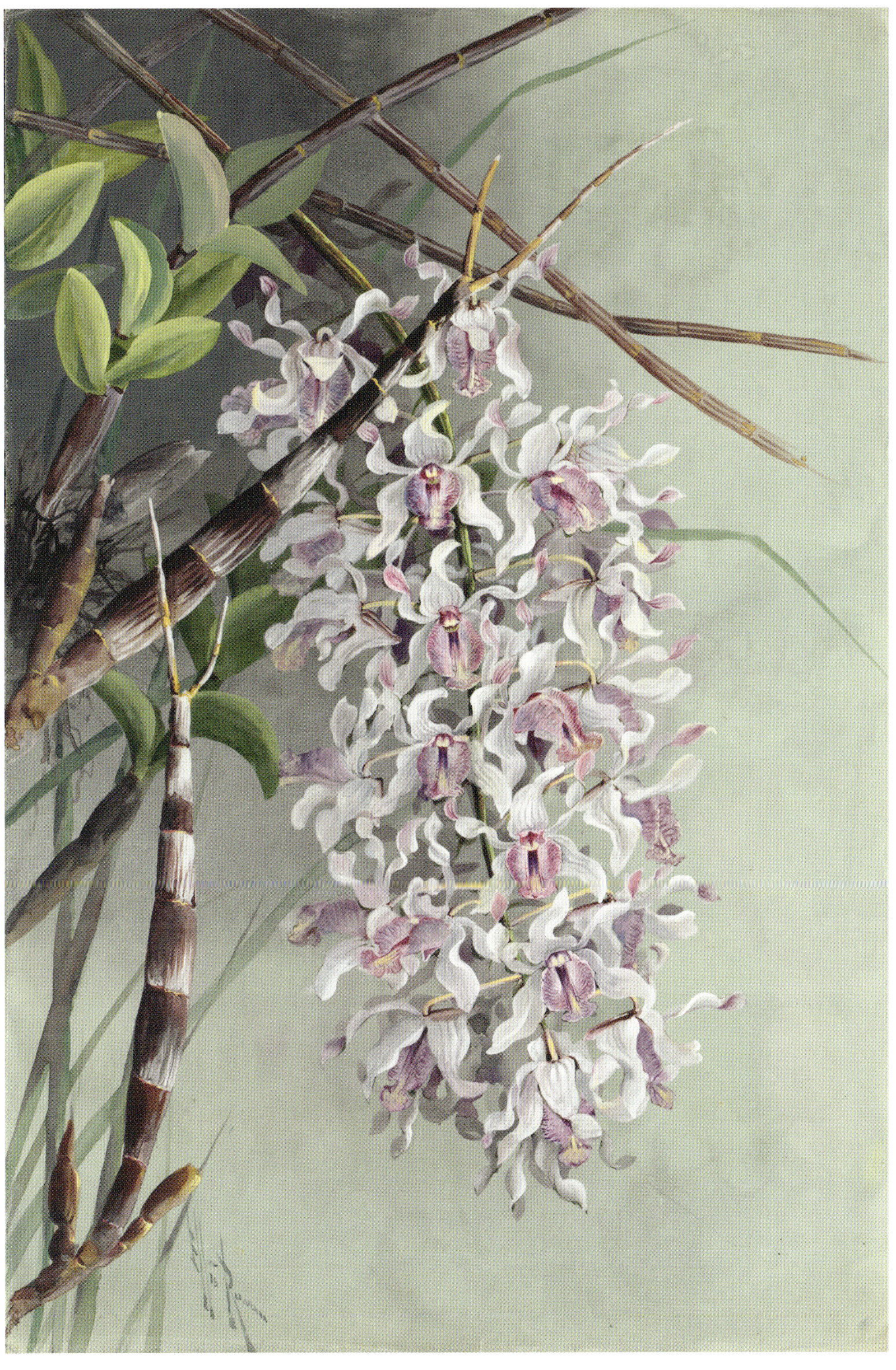

Blue Antler Orchid c.1887
gouache and watercolour on paper; 56 x 38 cm; Queensland
nla.cat-vn1321323

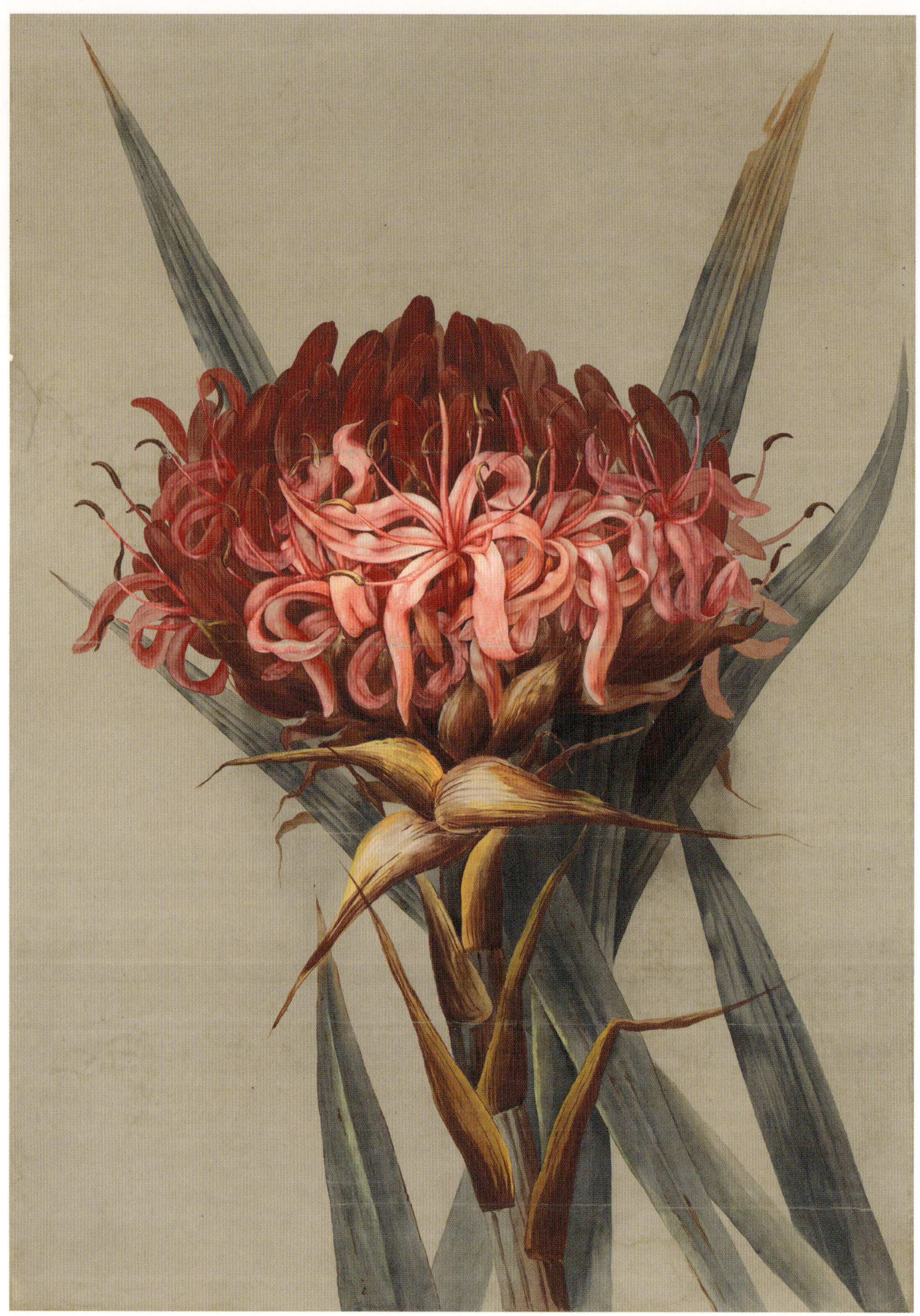

Gymea Lily c.1887–1889
gouache and watercolour on paper; 76.2 x 55 cm; New South Wales
nla.cat-vn542828

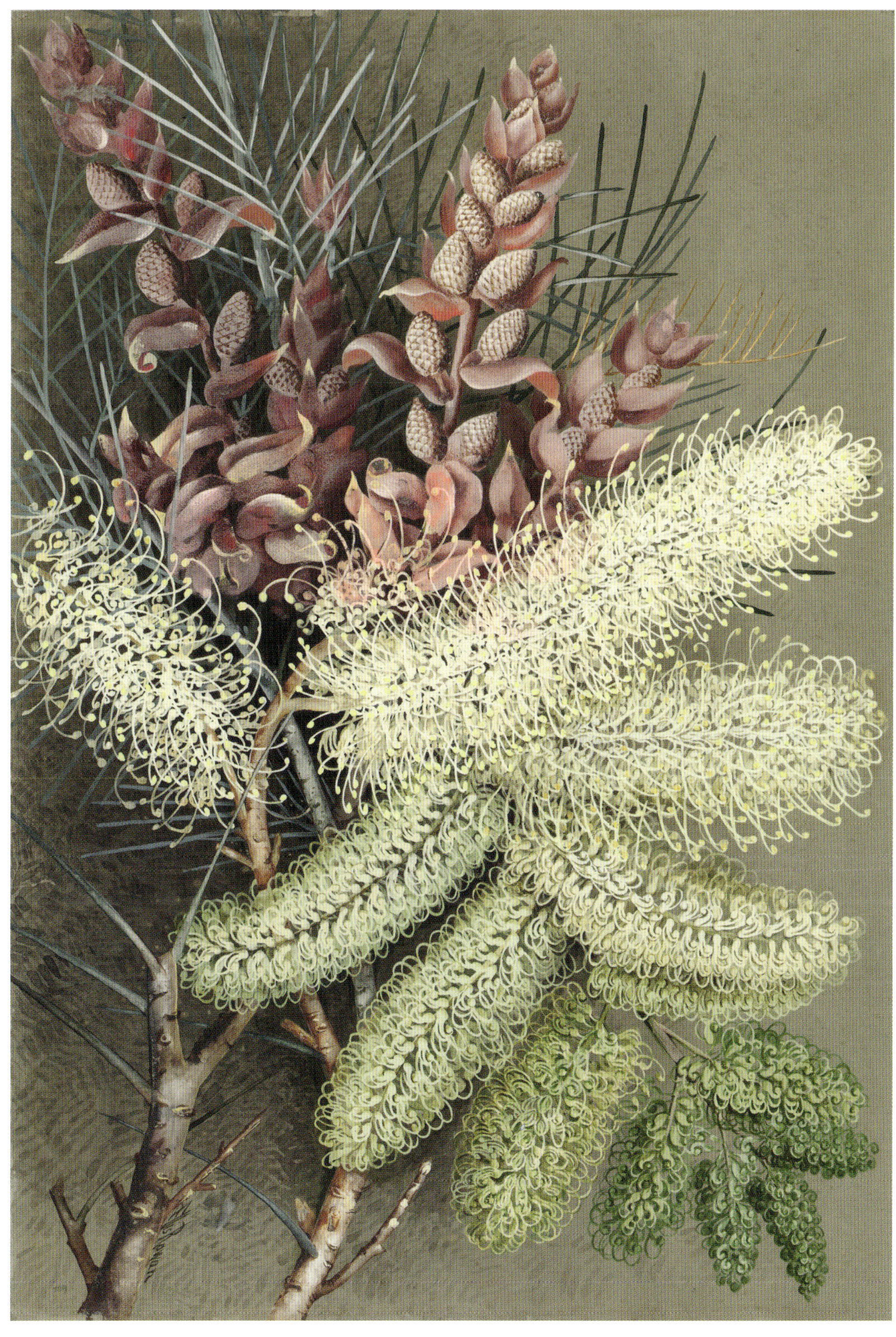

White Plume Grevillea c.1889
gouache and watercolour on paper; 53.3 x 35.5 cm; Western Australia
nla.cat-vn572396

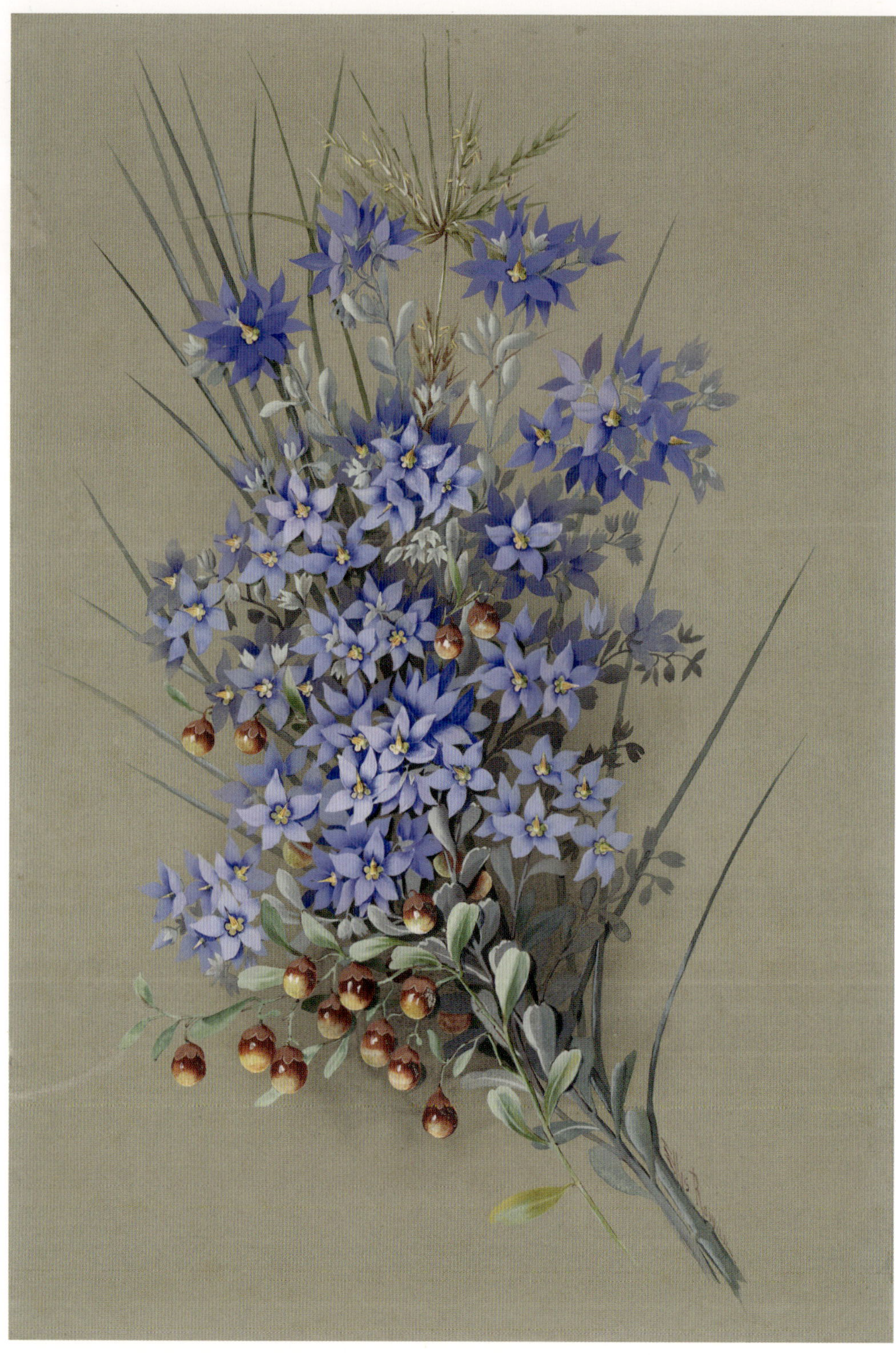

Beach Spinifex and Pebble Bush c.1889
gouache and watercolour on paper; 54 x 37.3 cm; Carnarvon, Western Australia
nla.cat-vn2843712

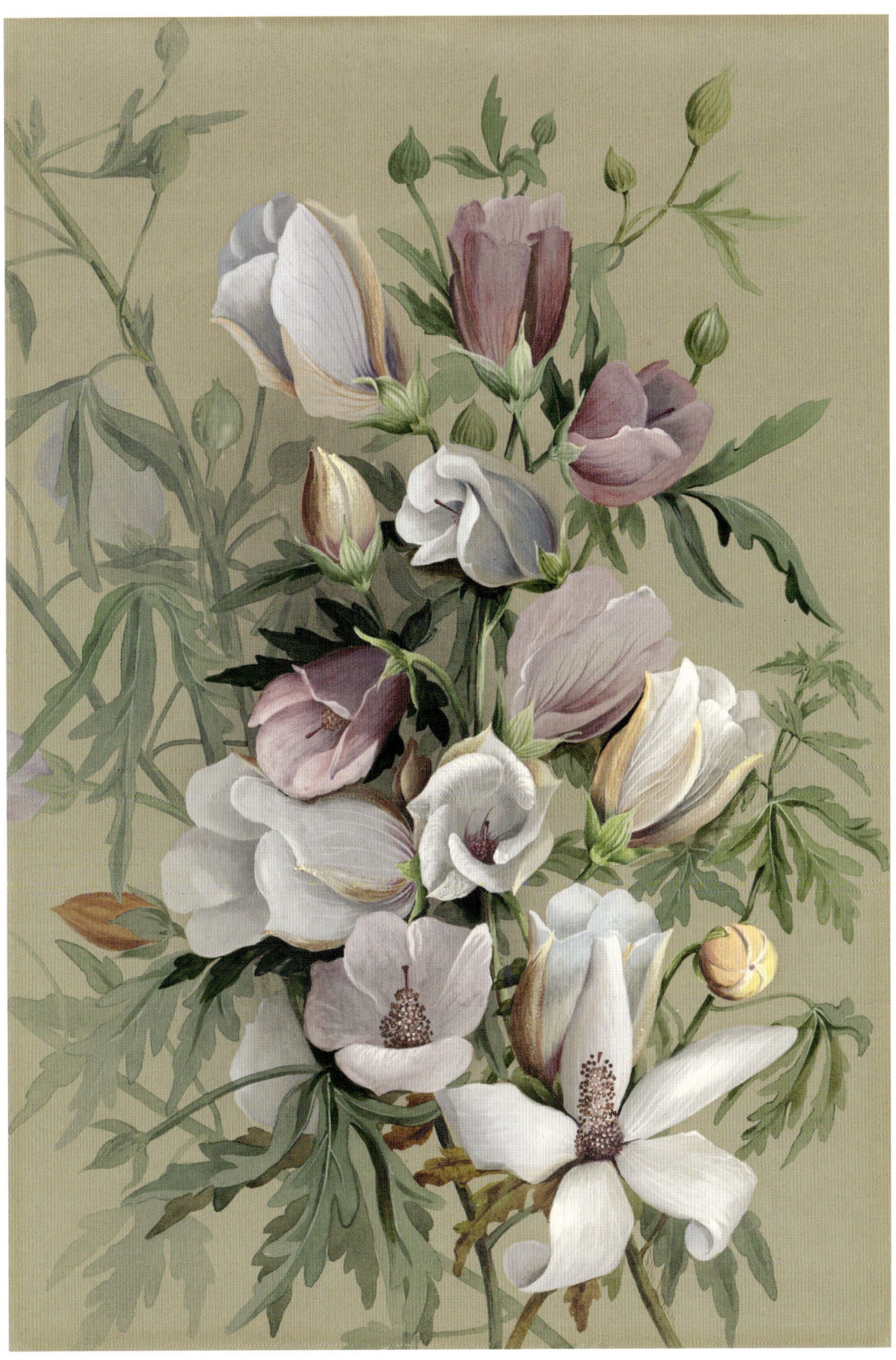

Lilac Hibiscus c.1889
gouache and watercolour on paper; 54.7 x 38 cm; Champion Bay, Western Australia
nla.cat-vn1327925

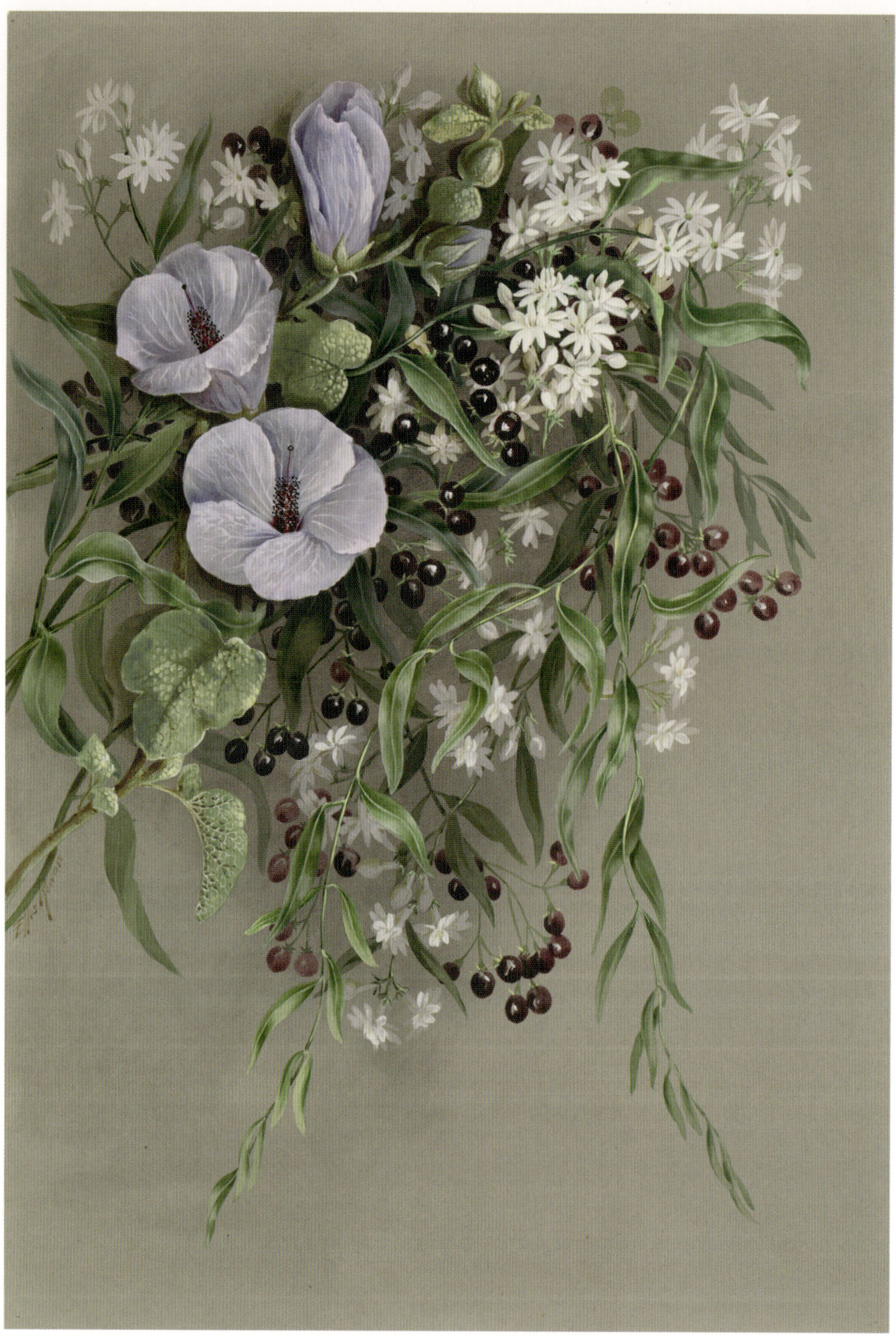

Native Hibiscus, Native Willow and Berries c.1889
gouache and watercolour on paper; 54.5 x 38 cm; Western Australia
nla.cat-vn1338073

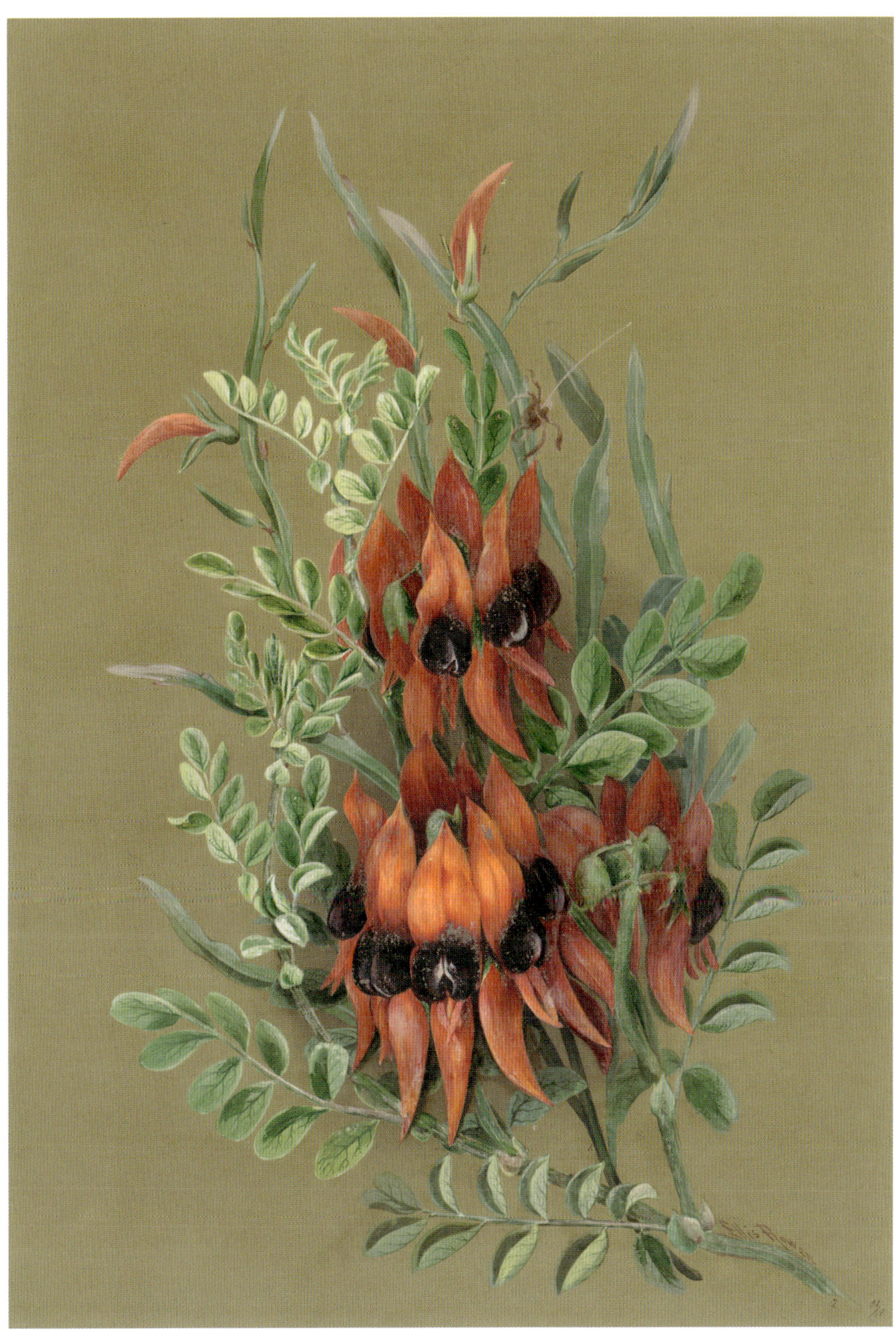

Sturt's Desert Pea c.1889
gouache and watercolour on paper; 54.5 x 38 cm; Western Australia
nla.cat-vn1317560

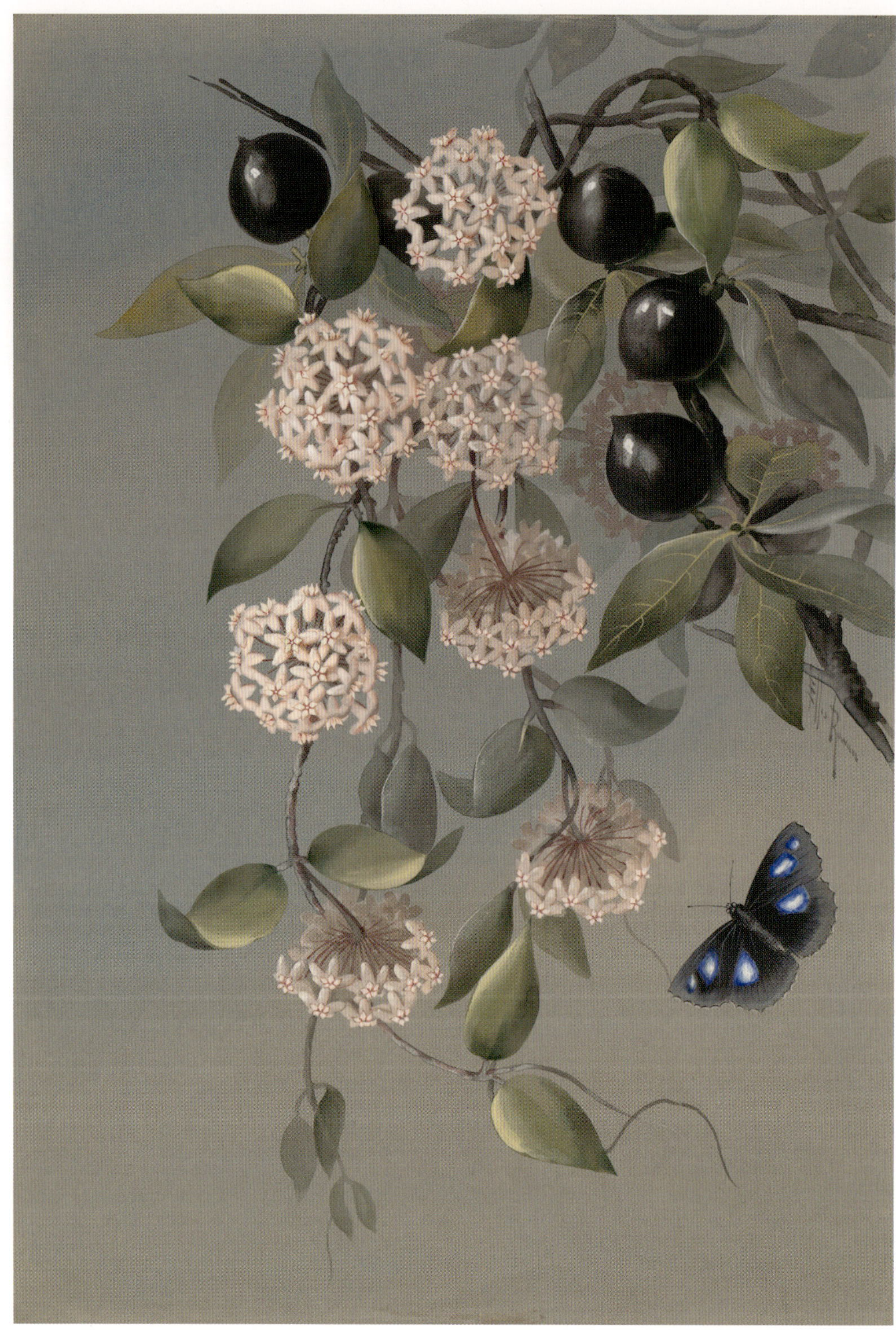

Native Hoya and Brown Pearwood c.1880s
gouache and watercolour on paper; 54.7 x 38 cm; Queensland
nla.cat-vn2839607

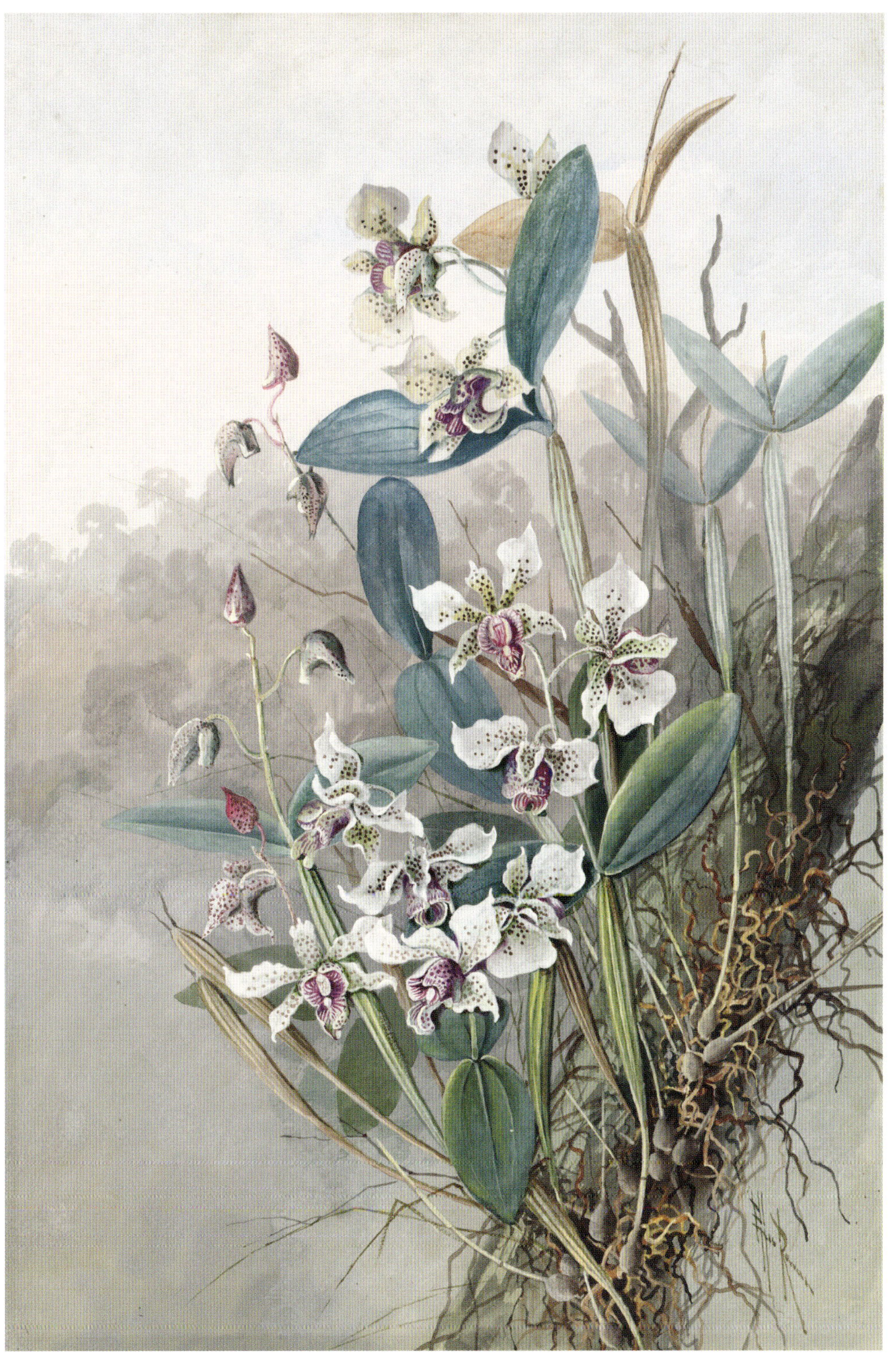

Tree Orchid and Forest, c.1890–1892
gouache and watercolour on paper; 55.7 x 38 cm; Queensland
nla.cat-vn214514

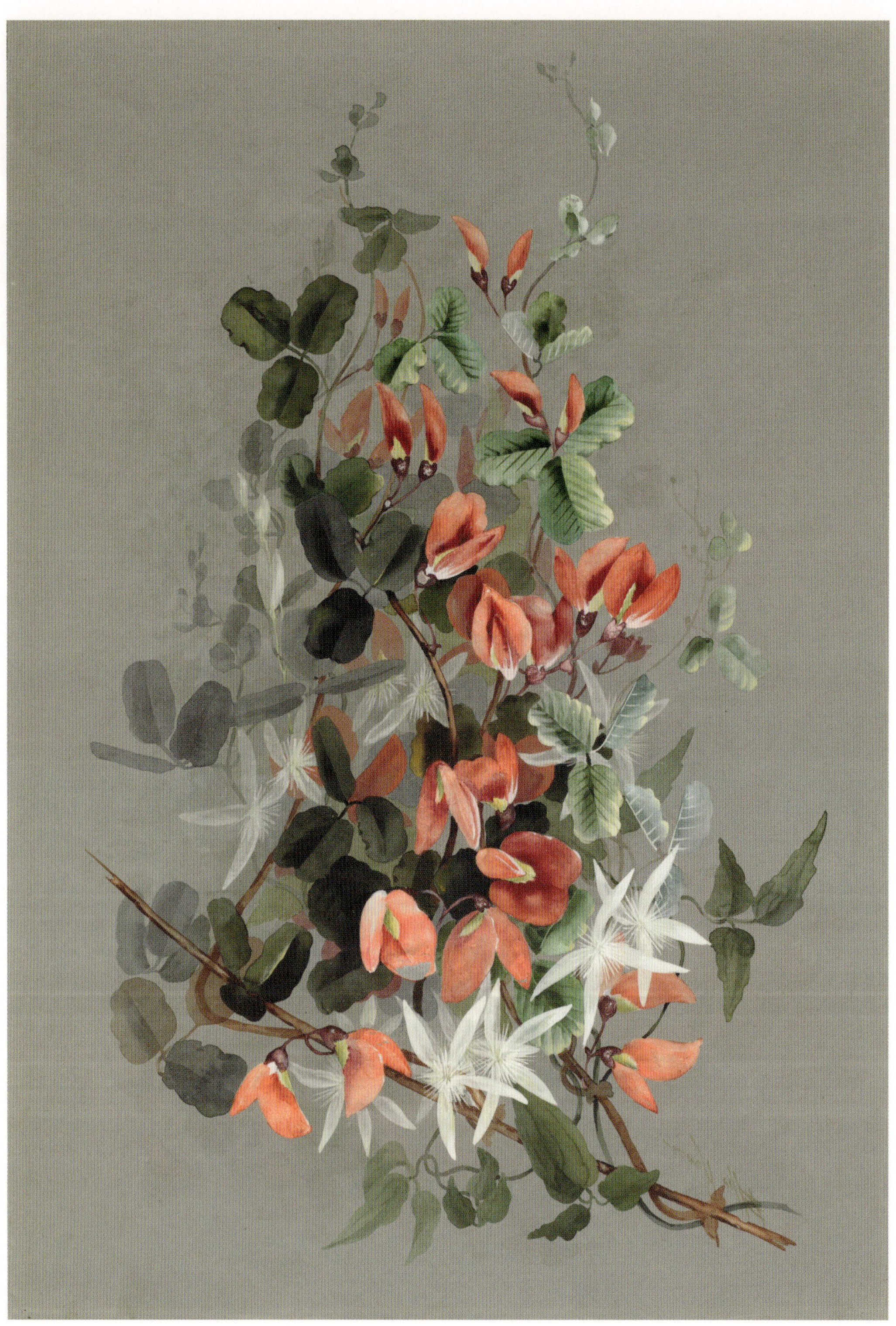

Old Man's Beard and Running Postman c.1891
gouache and watercolour on paper; 54.8 x 38 cm
nla.cat-vn1167359

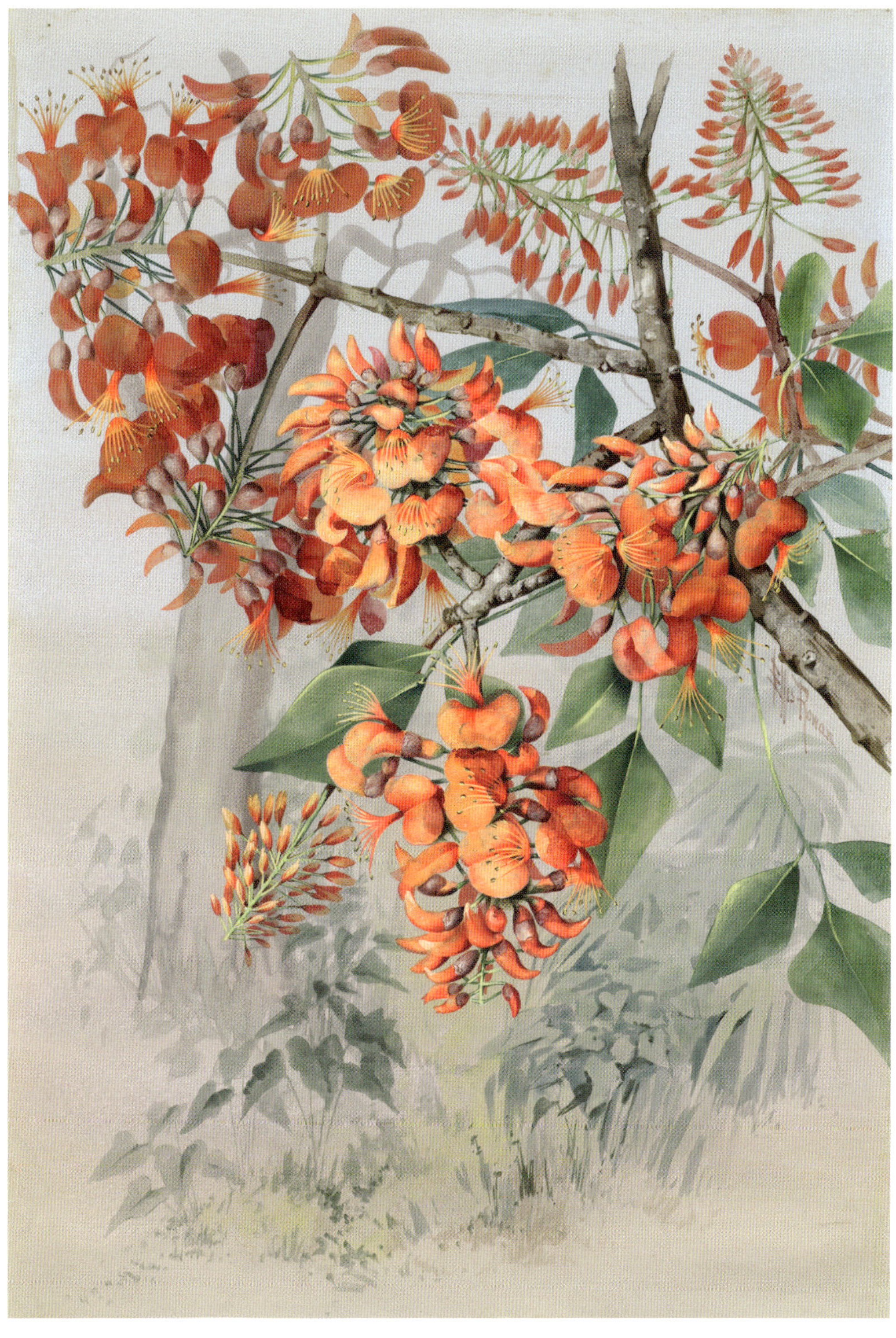

Bulswing Coral Tree c.1891
gouache and watercolour on paper; 54.5 x 37.5 cm; Somerset, Queensland
nla.cat-vn2683547

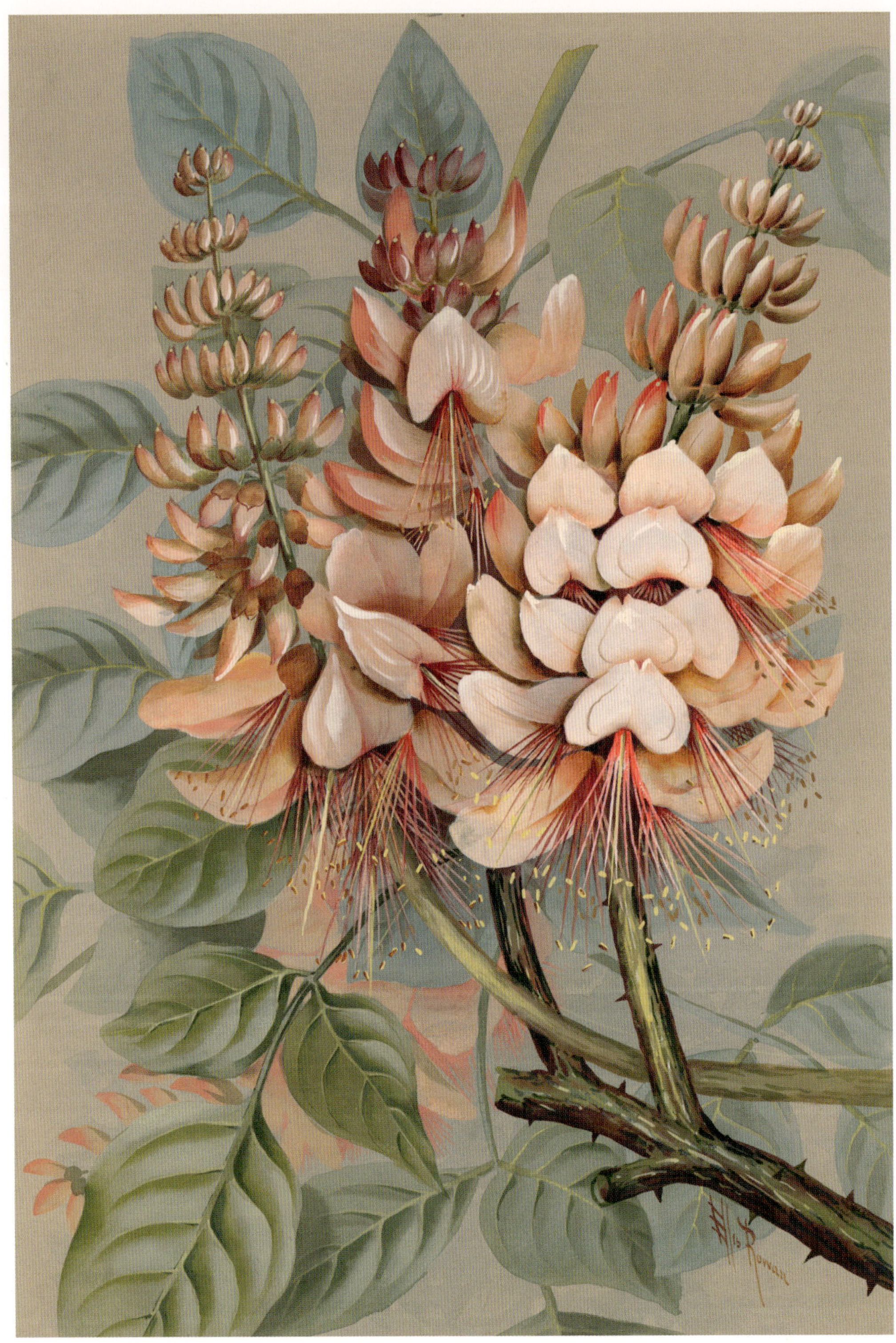

Indian Coral Tree c.1891
gouache and watercolour on paper; 54.5 x 37.7 cm; Queensland
nla.cat-vn1317791

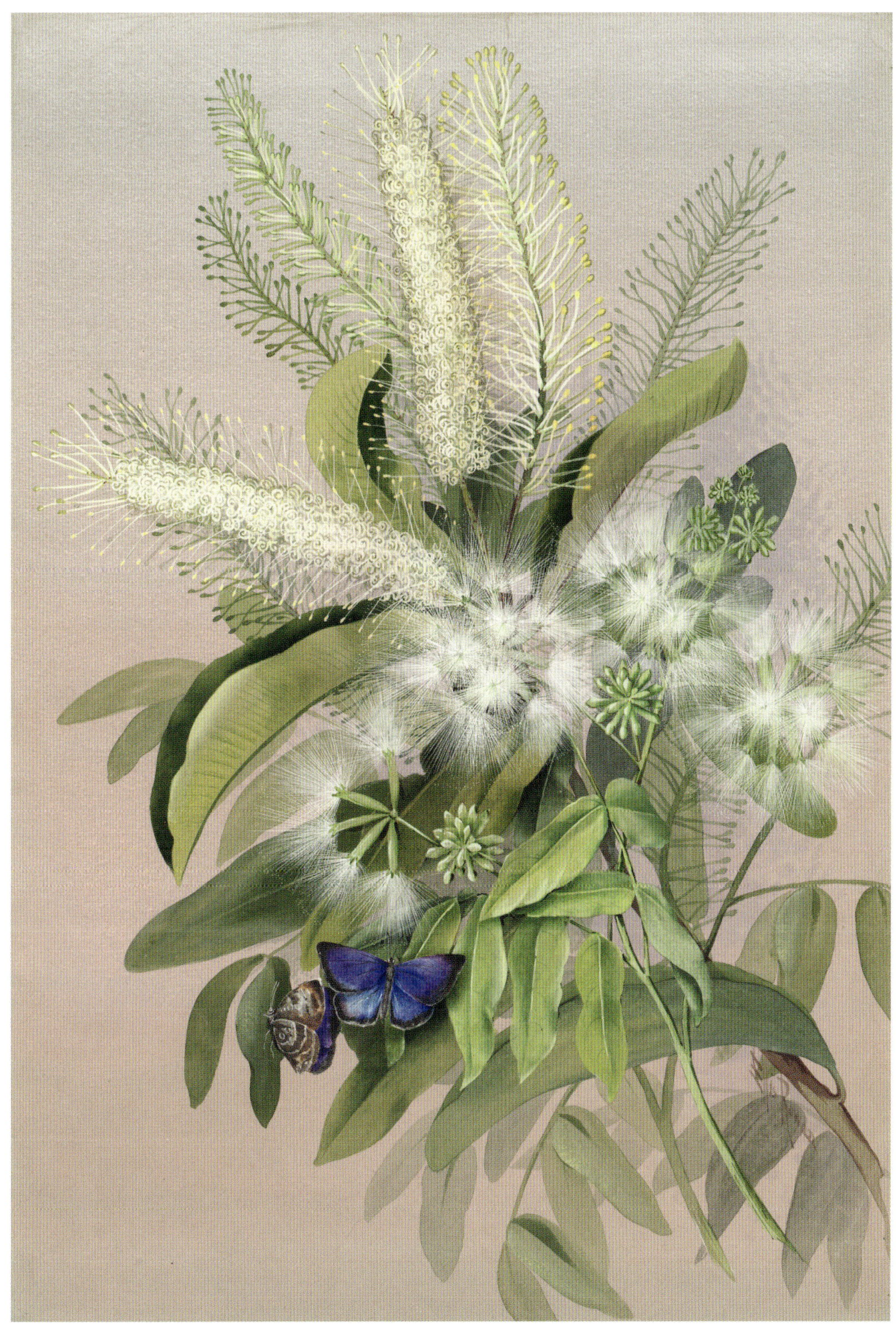

Snowwood and Queensland Nut c.1892
gouache and watercolour on paper; 54.8 x 38.2 cm; Gertrude River, Queensland
nla.cat-vn2689477

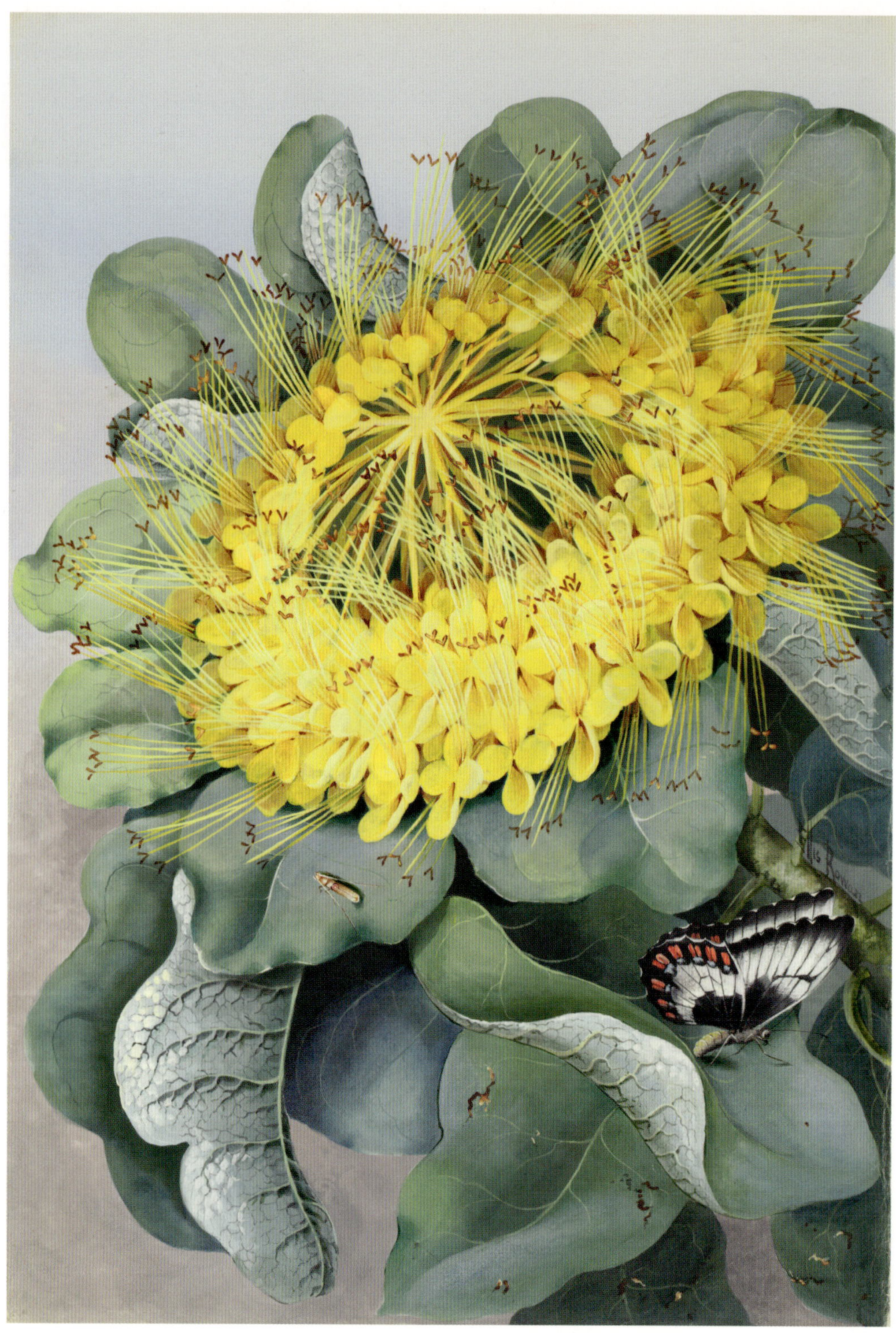

Golden Bouquet Tree c.1892
gouache and watercolour on paper; 54.5 x 38 cm; Somerset, Queensland
nla.cat-vn226237

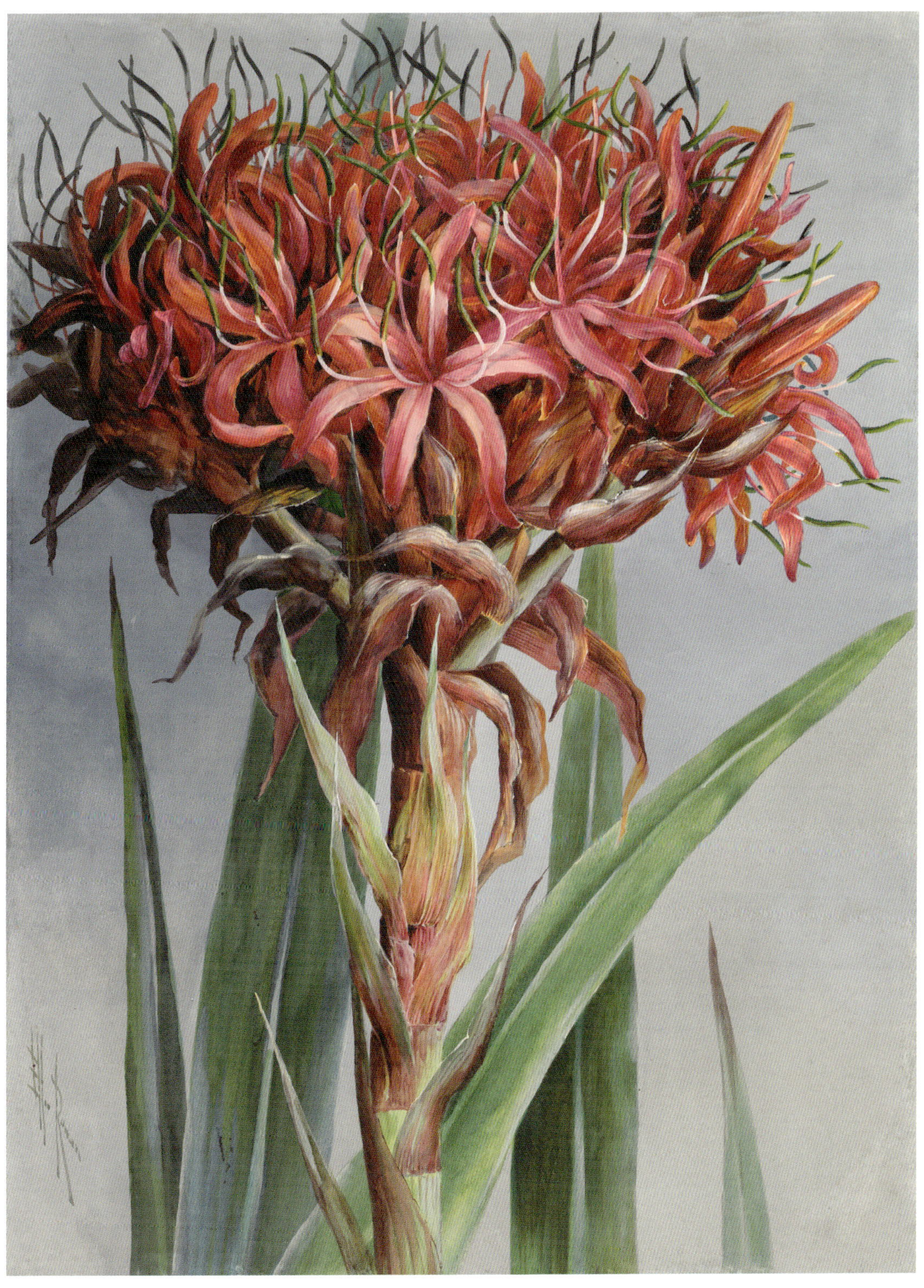

Gymea Lily c.1892
gouache and watercolour on paper; 76 x 56.2 cm; New South Wales
nla.cat-vn542769

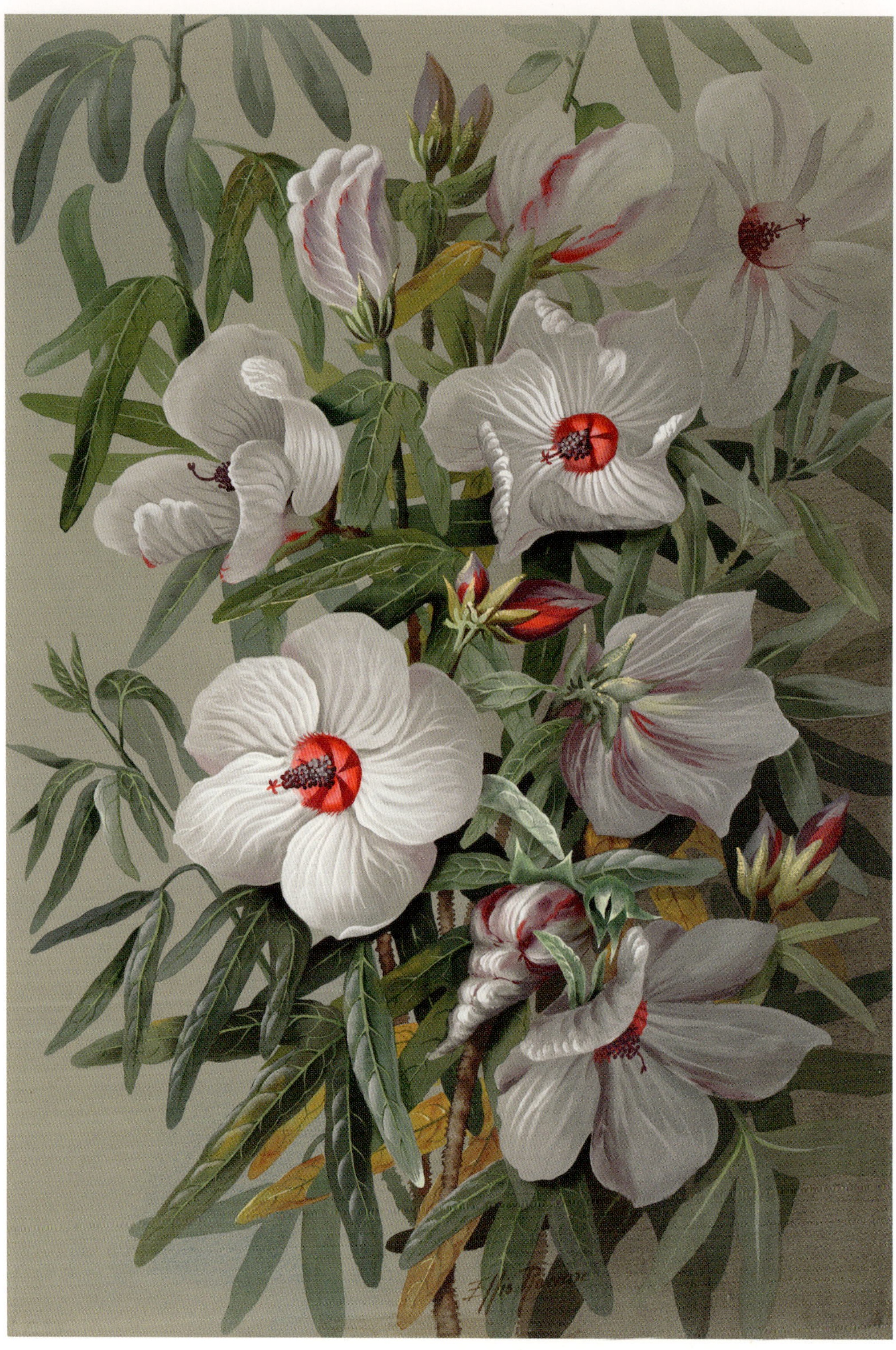

Native Rosella c.1892
gouache and watercolour on paper; 55 x 38 cm; New South Wales
nla.cat-vn1319598

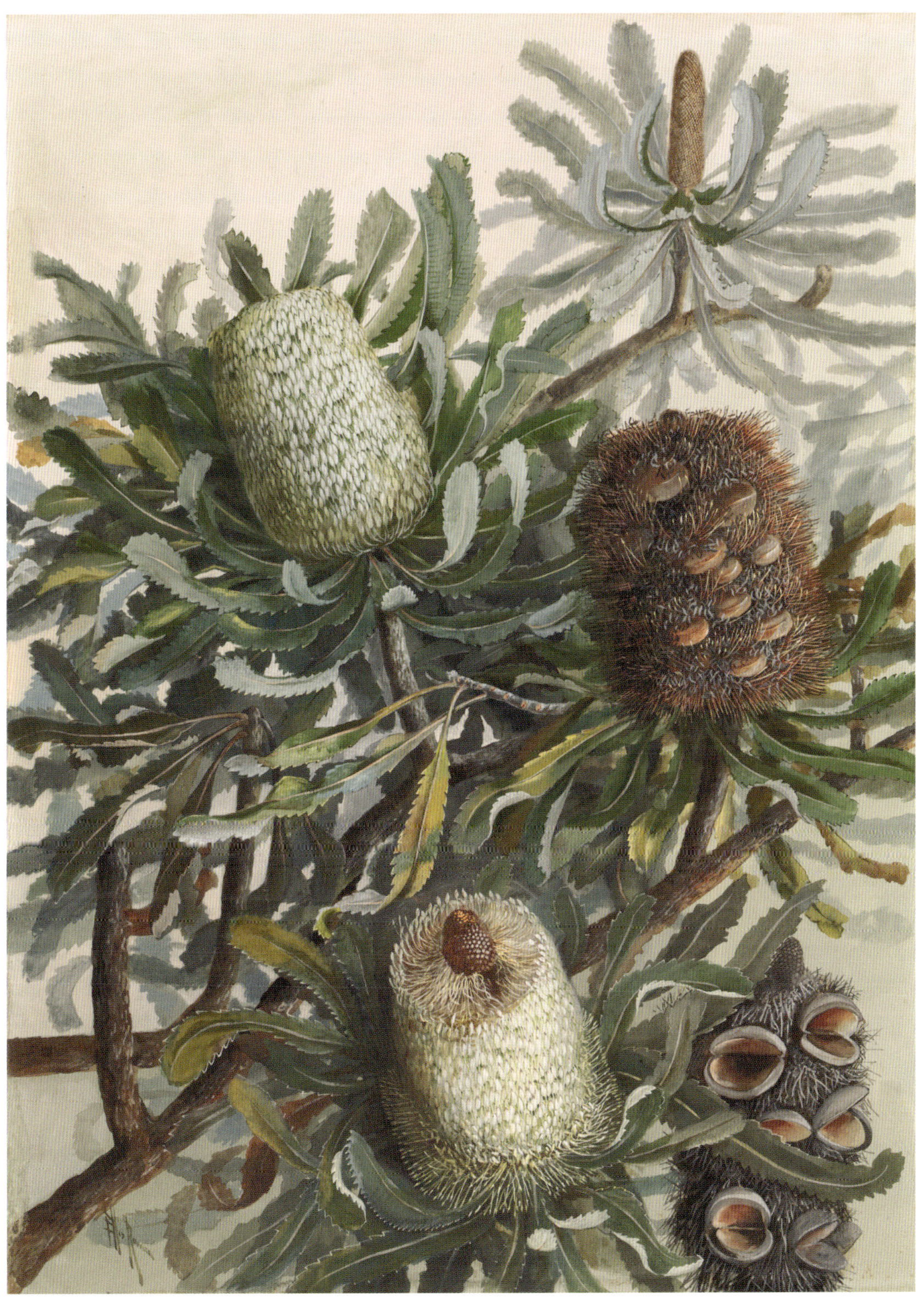

Saw Banksia c.1892
gouache and watercolour on paper; 76 x 56.2 cm; Queensland
nla.cat-vn542809

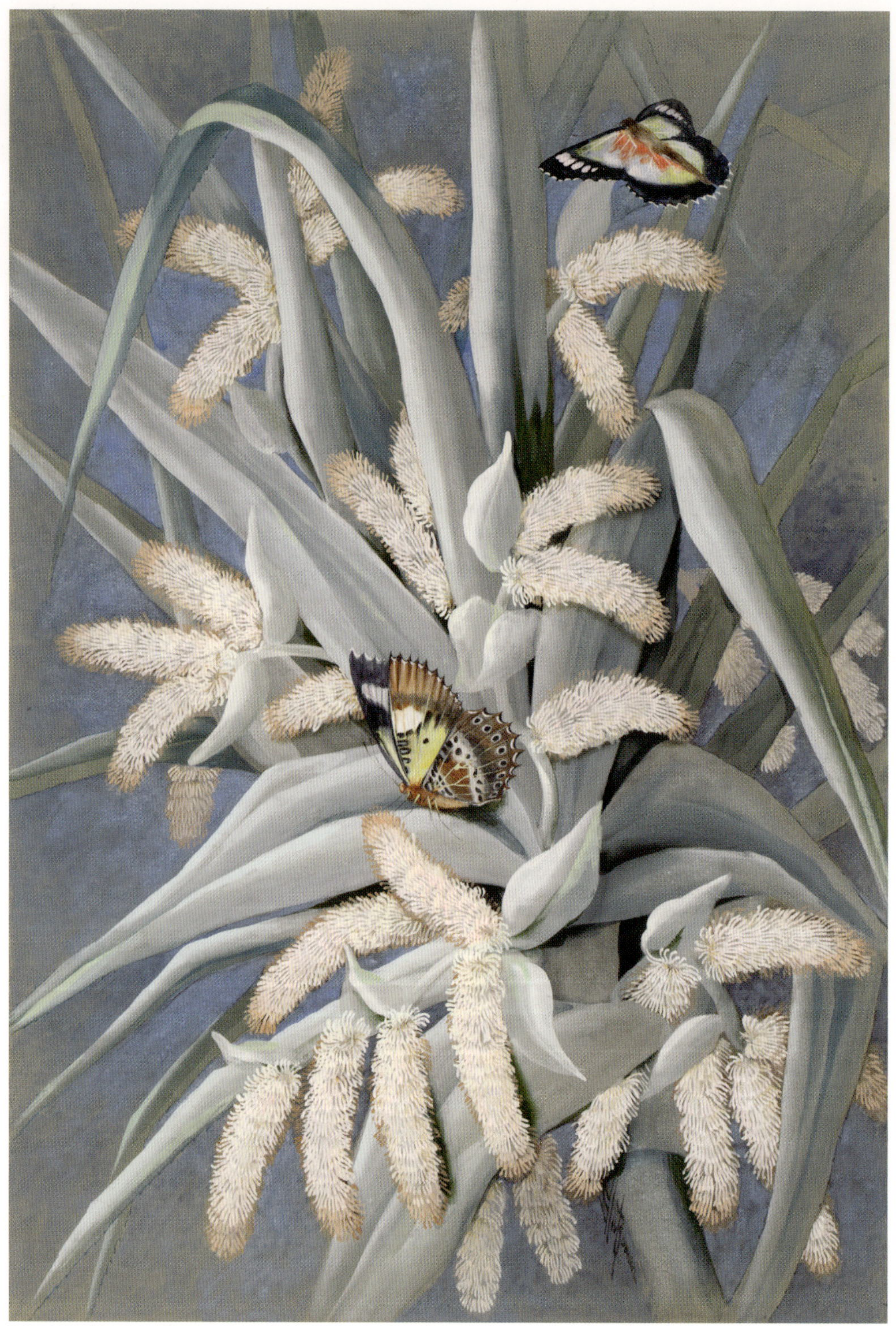

Screw Pine c.1892
gouache and watercolour on paper; 54.5 x 38 cm; Johnstone River, Queensland
nla.cat-vn2845021

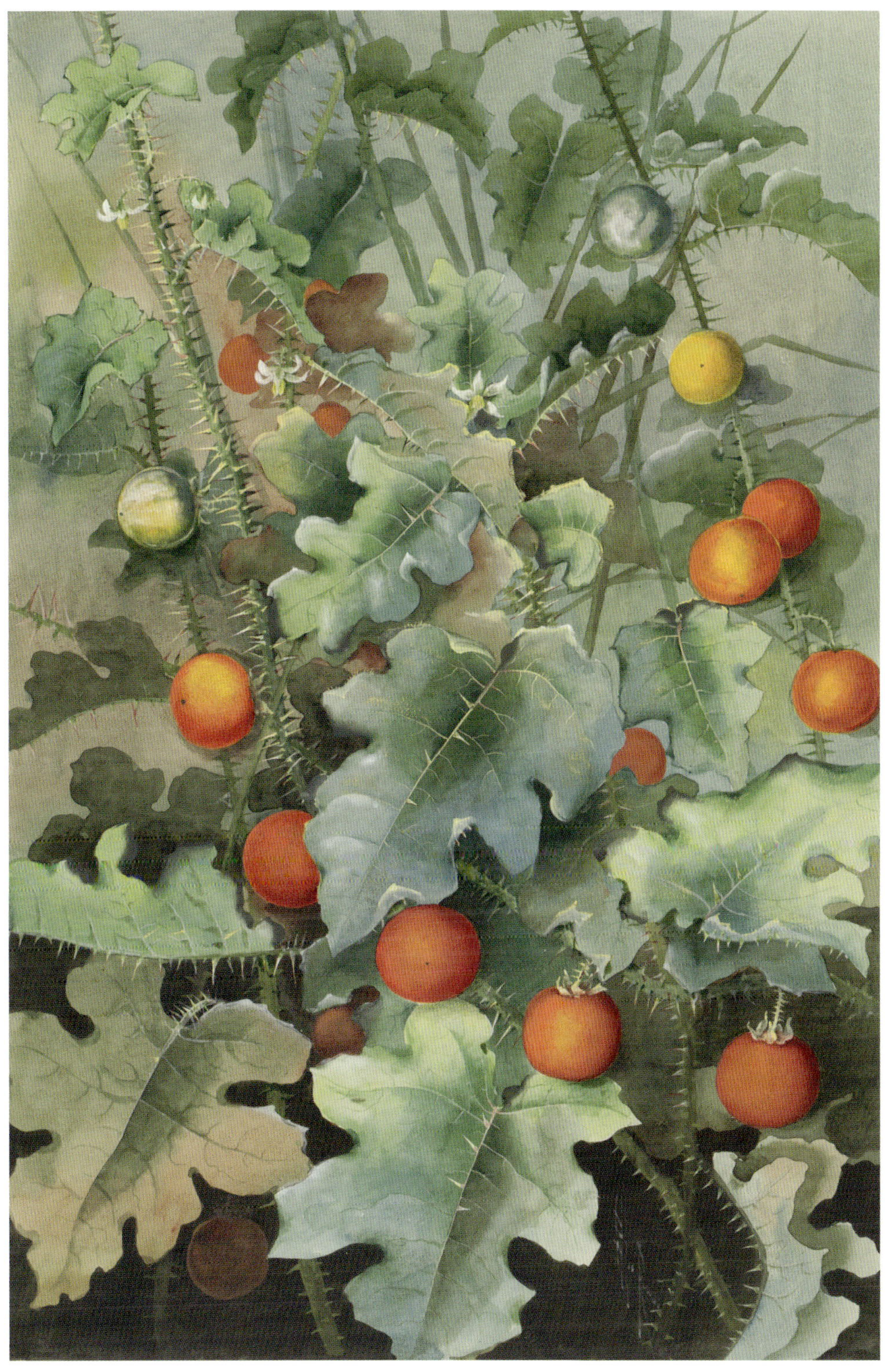

Devil's Apple c.1892
gouache and watercolour on paper; 56 x 37.6 cm; Queensland
nla.cat-vn2838924

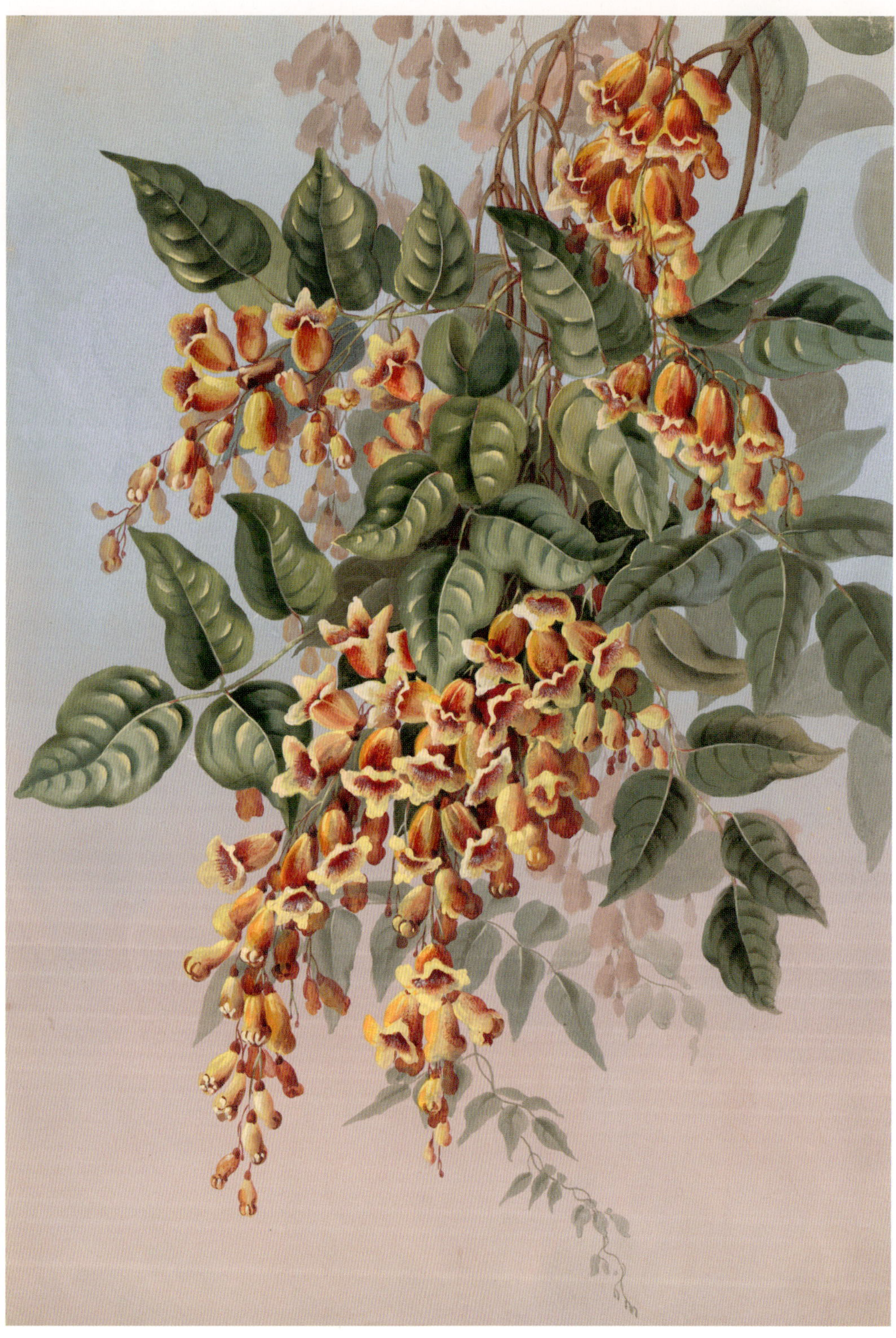

Wonga Wonga Vine c.1892
gouache and watercolour on paper; 54.7 x 38 cm
nla.cat-vn2868315

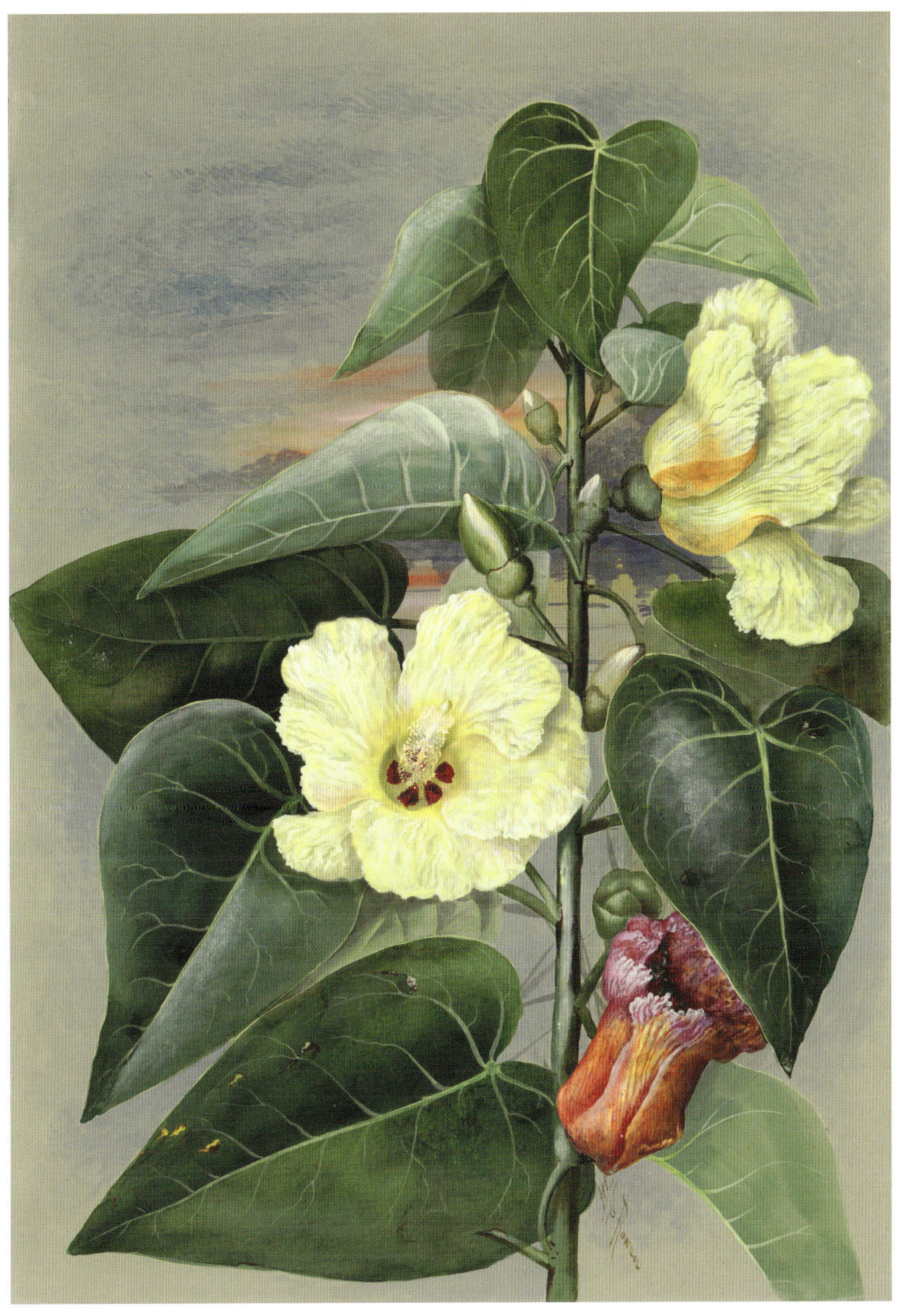

Portia Tree of Pacific Rosewood 1892
gouache and watercolour on paper; 54.5 x 38 cm; Bloomfield, Queensland
nla.cat-vn2840257

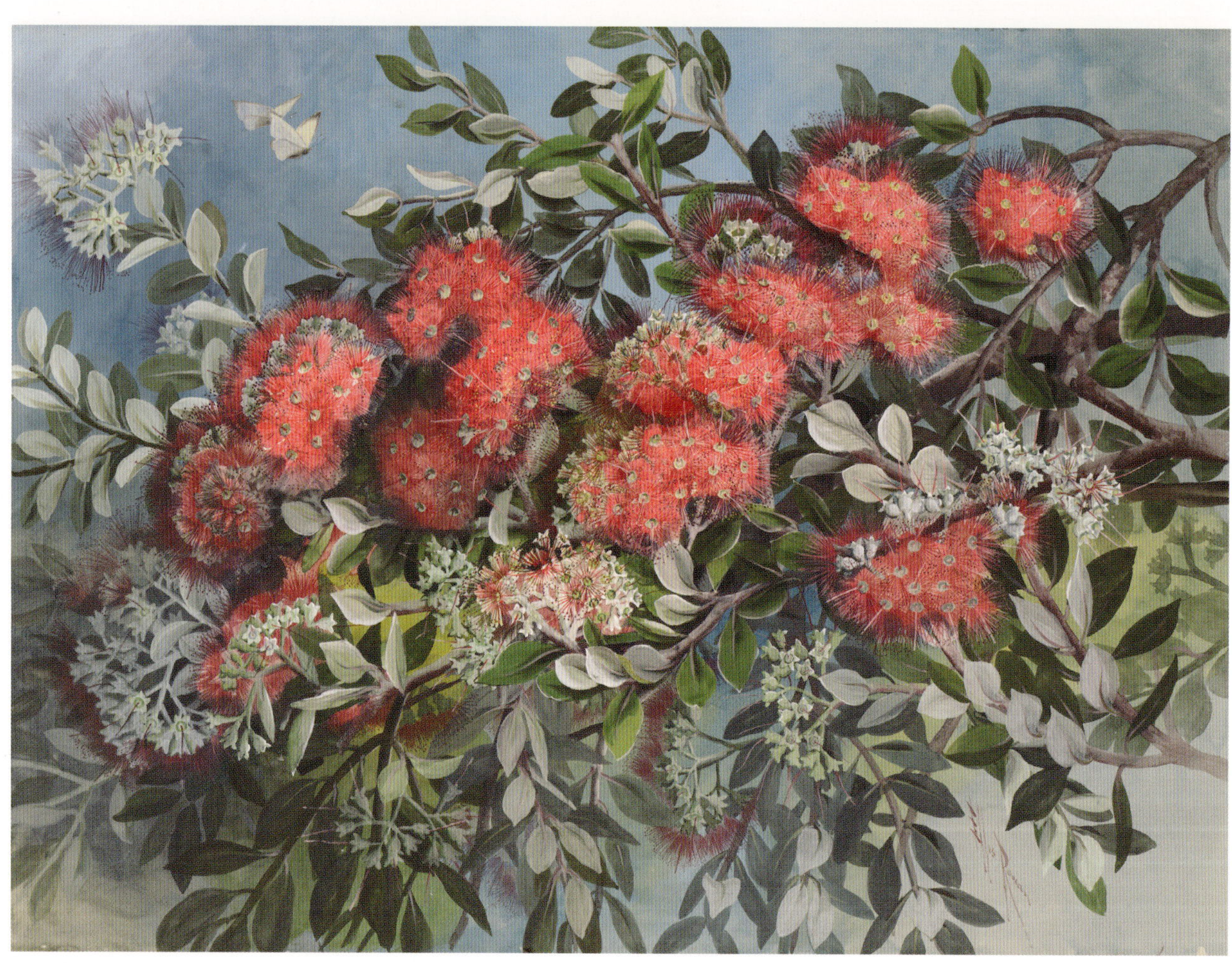

New Zealand Christmas Bush c.1893
gouache and watercolour on paper; 56.2 x 76 cm; New Zealand
nla.cat-vn1737015

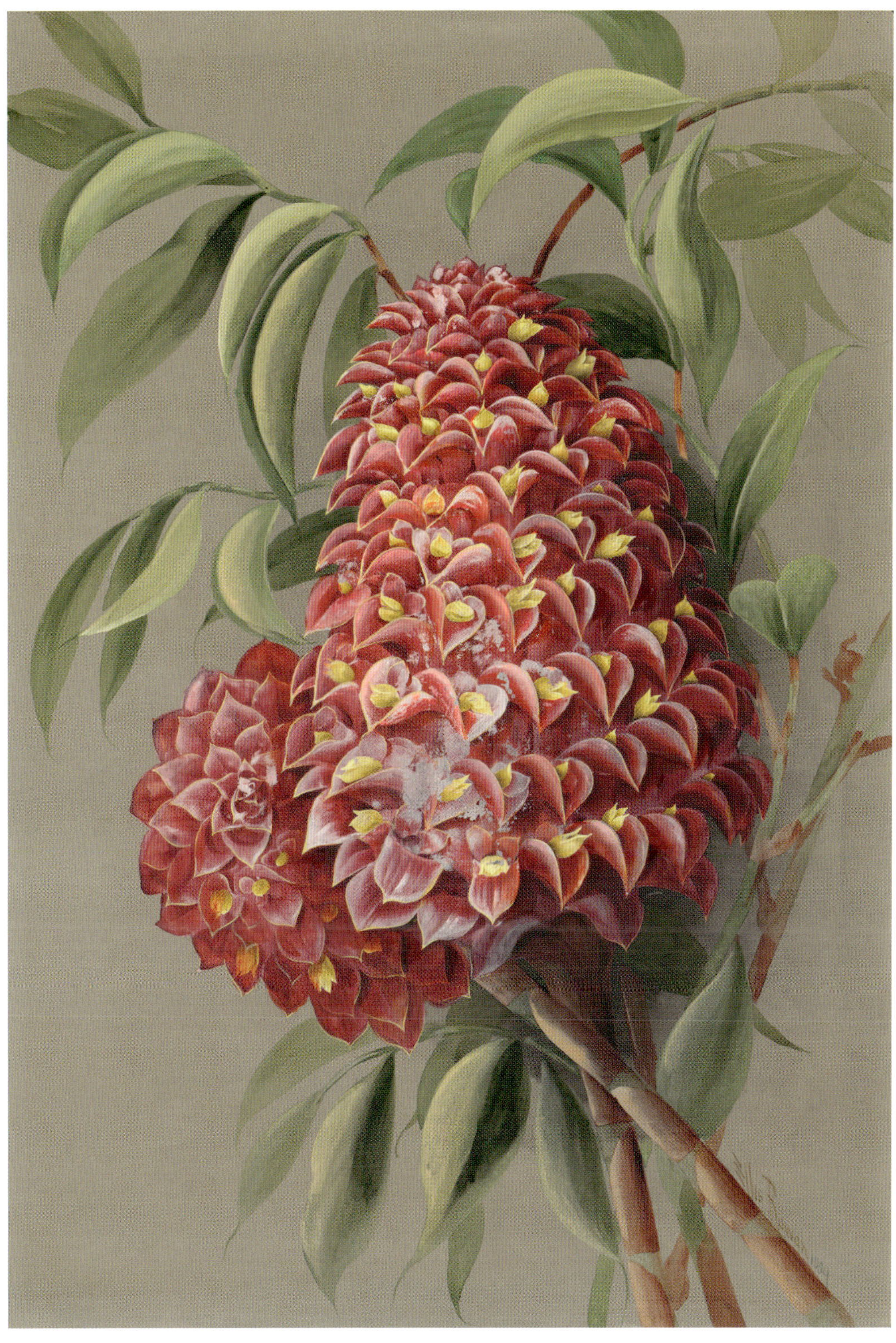

Pineapple Ginger 1897
gouache and watercolour on paper; 54.8 x 38 cm; Johnstone River, Queensland
nla.cat-vn2689381

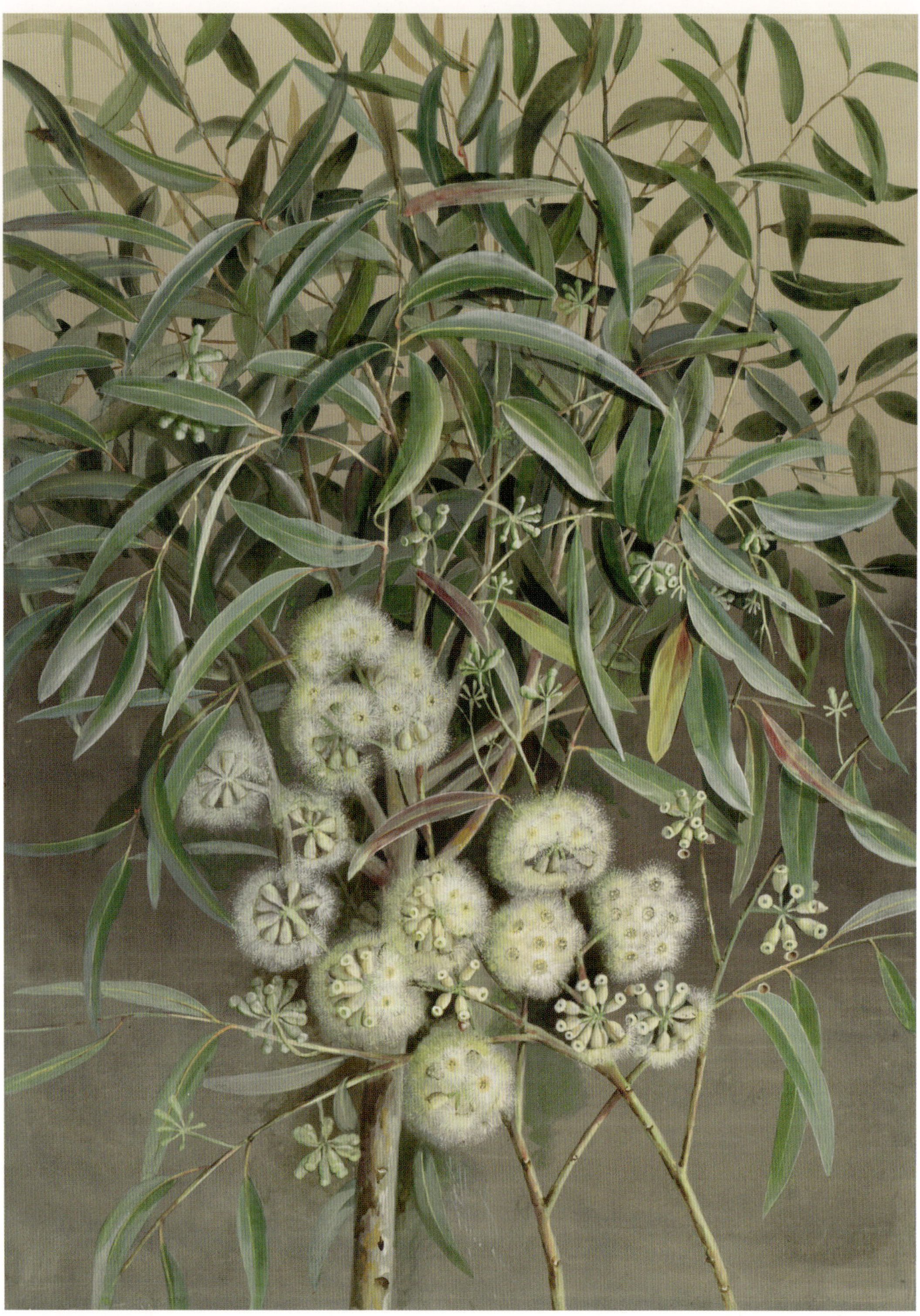

Sugar Gum c.1906
gouache and watercolour on paper; 73.4 x 54 cm; South Australia
nla.cat-vn2065101

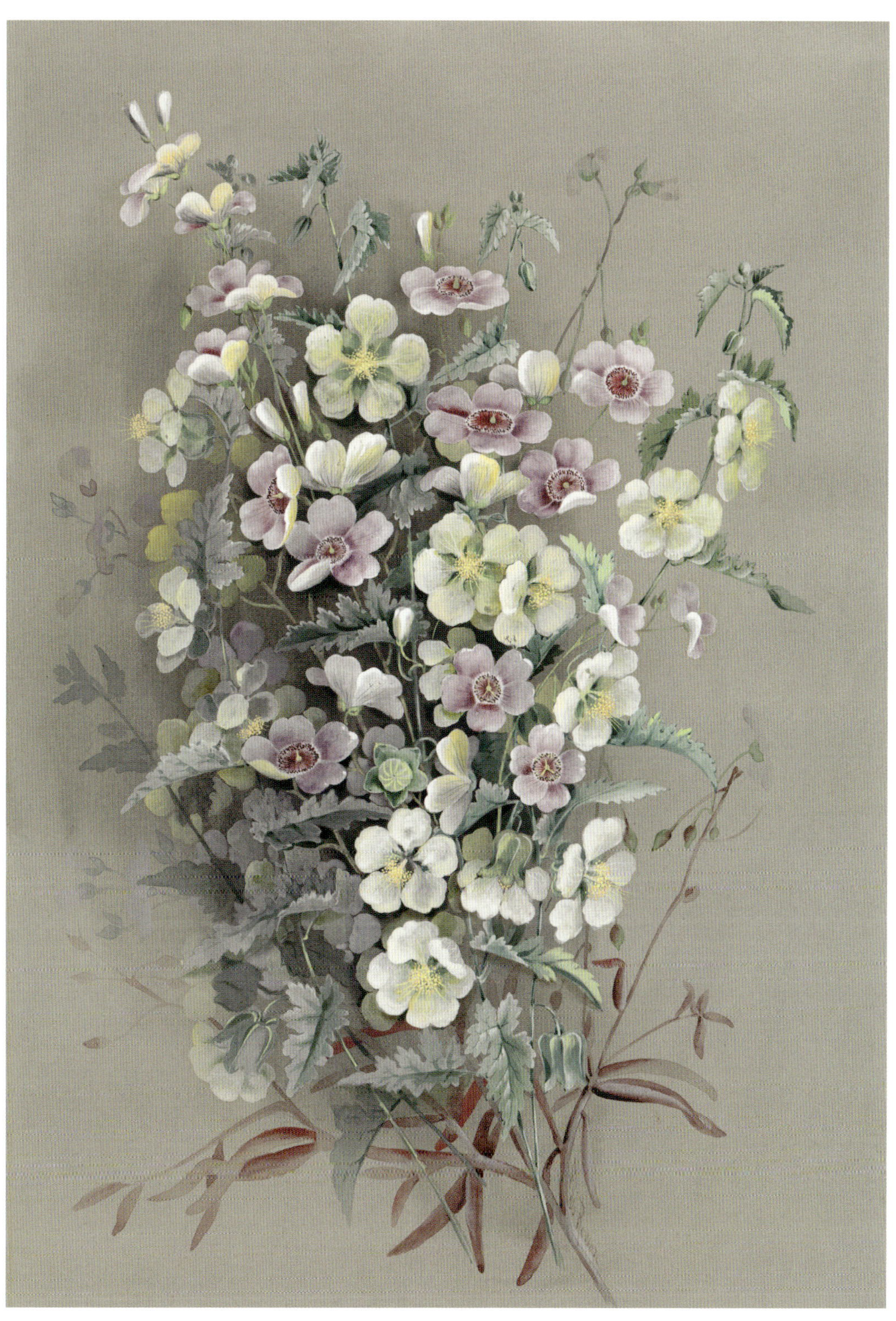

Parakeelya and Flannel Weed c.1906
gouache and watercolour on paper; 54.5 x 37.8 cm; Western Australia
nla.cat-vn1167352

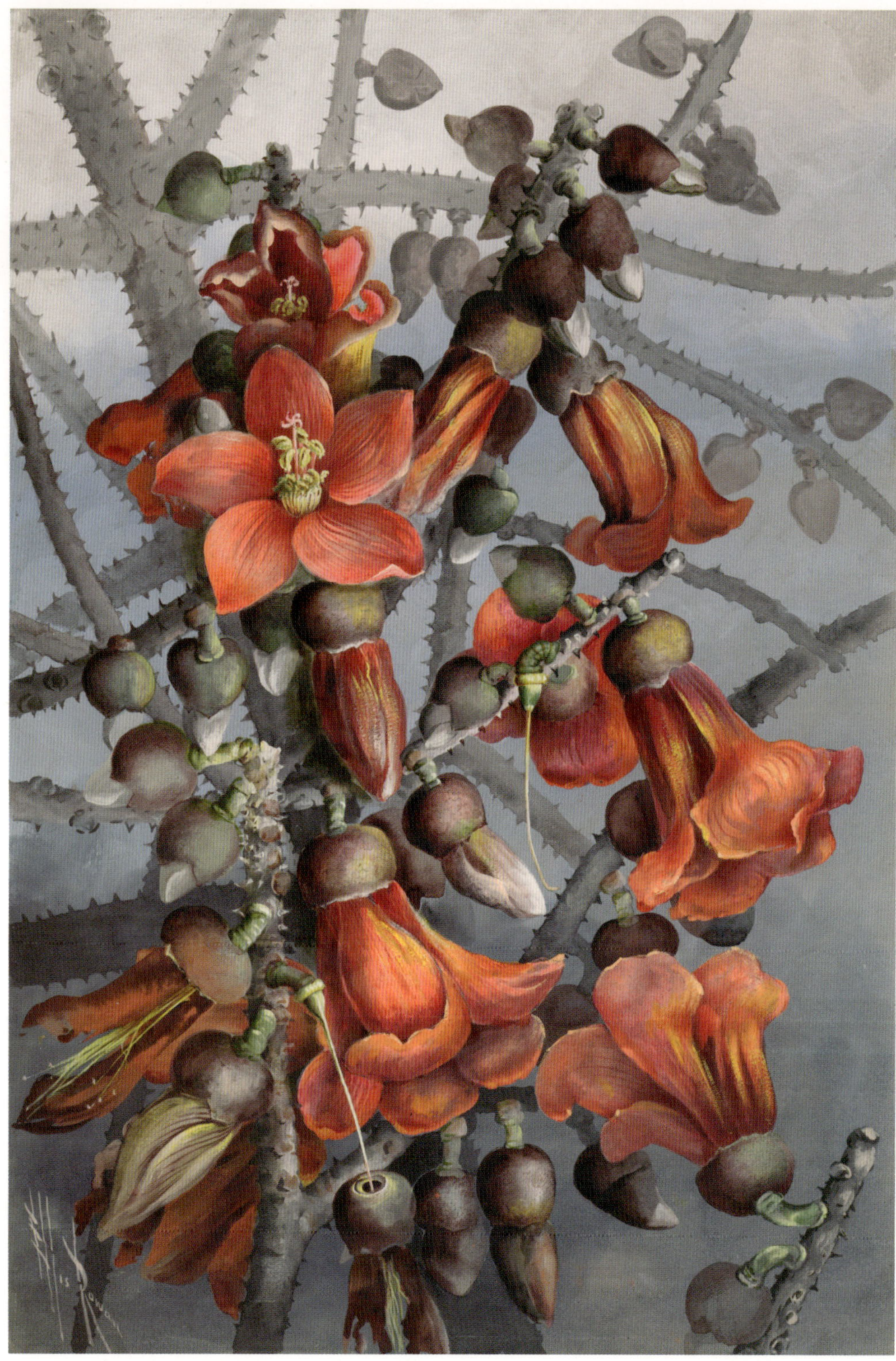

Red Silk Cotton Tree c.1911
gouache and watercolour on paper; 56 x 38.2 cm; Queensland
nla.cat-vn2845197

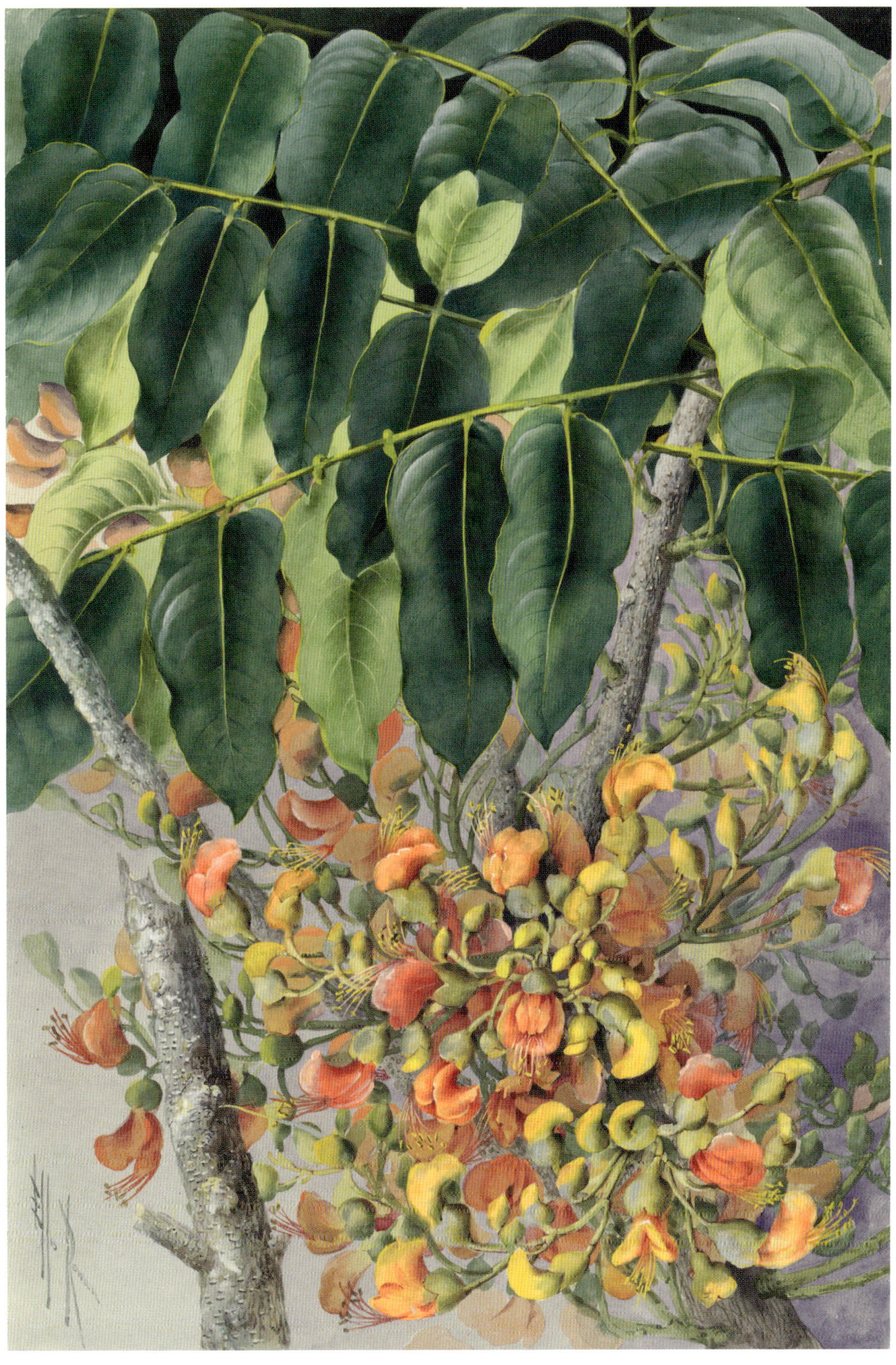

Moreton Bay Chestnut c.1911
gouache and watercolour on paper; 56 x 38 cm; Queensland
nla.cat-vn2848487

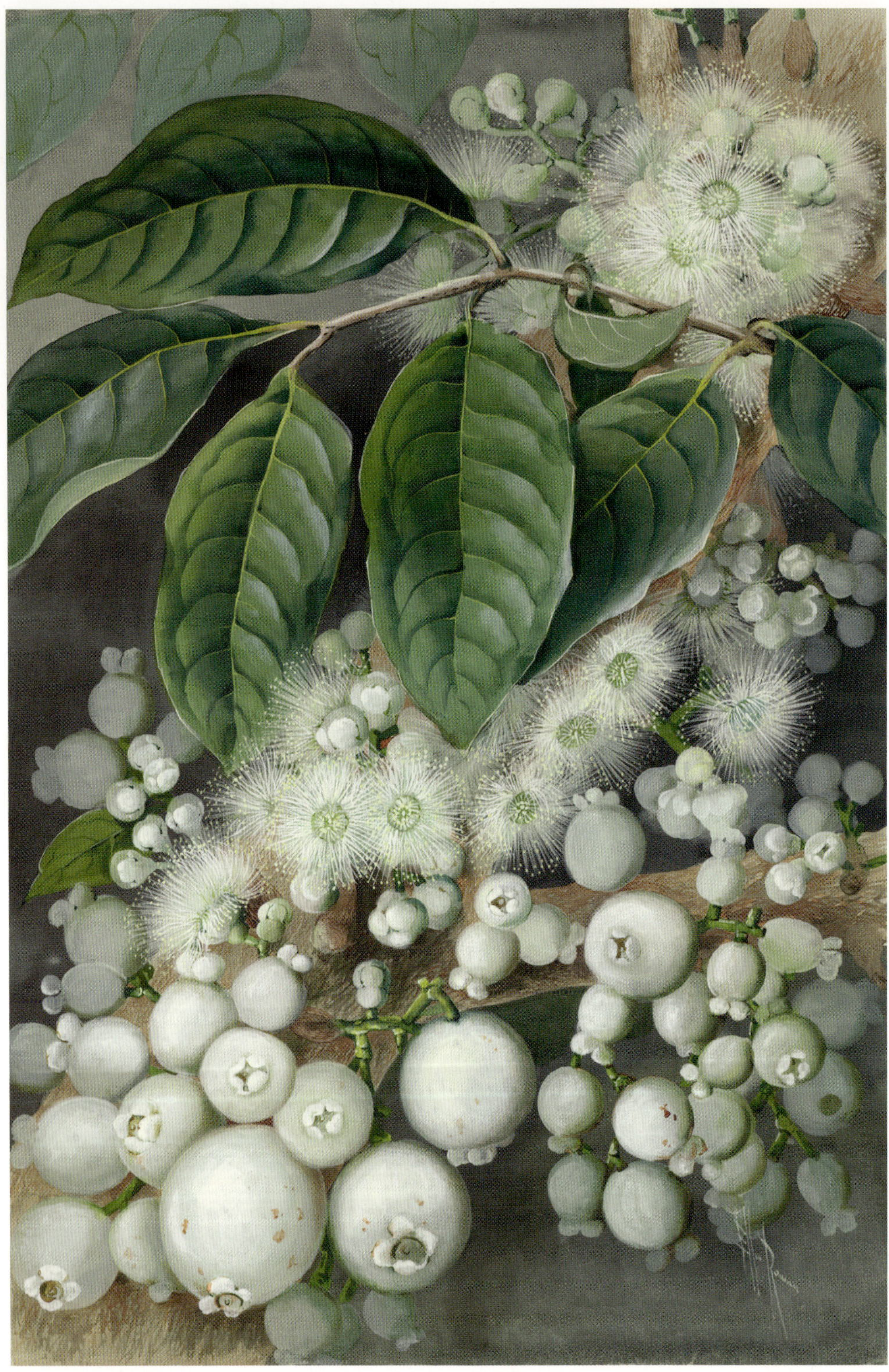

Wild or White Apple c.1911
gouache and watercolour on paper; 56 x 38 cm; Barron River, Queensland
nla.cat-vn2843660

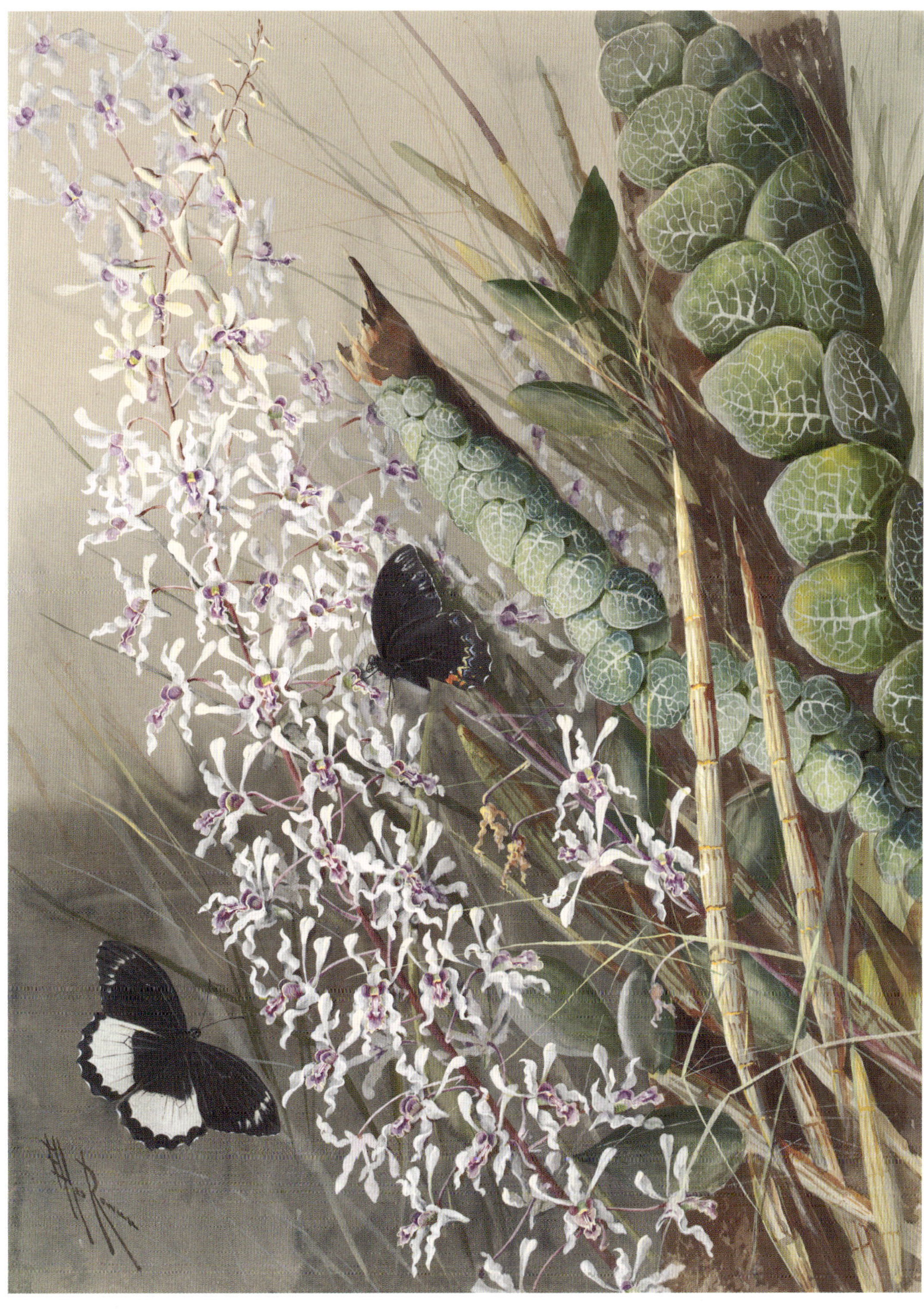

Large Tree Orchid with Papilio c.1911
gouache and watercolour on paper; 76.2 x 56 cm; Queensland
nla.cat-vn1736987

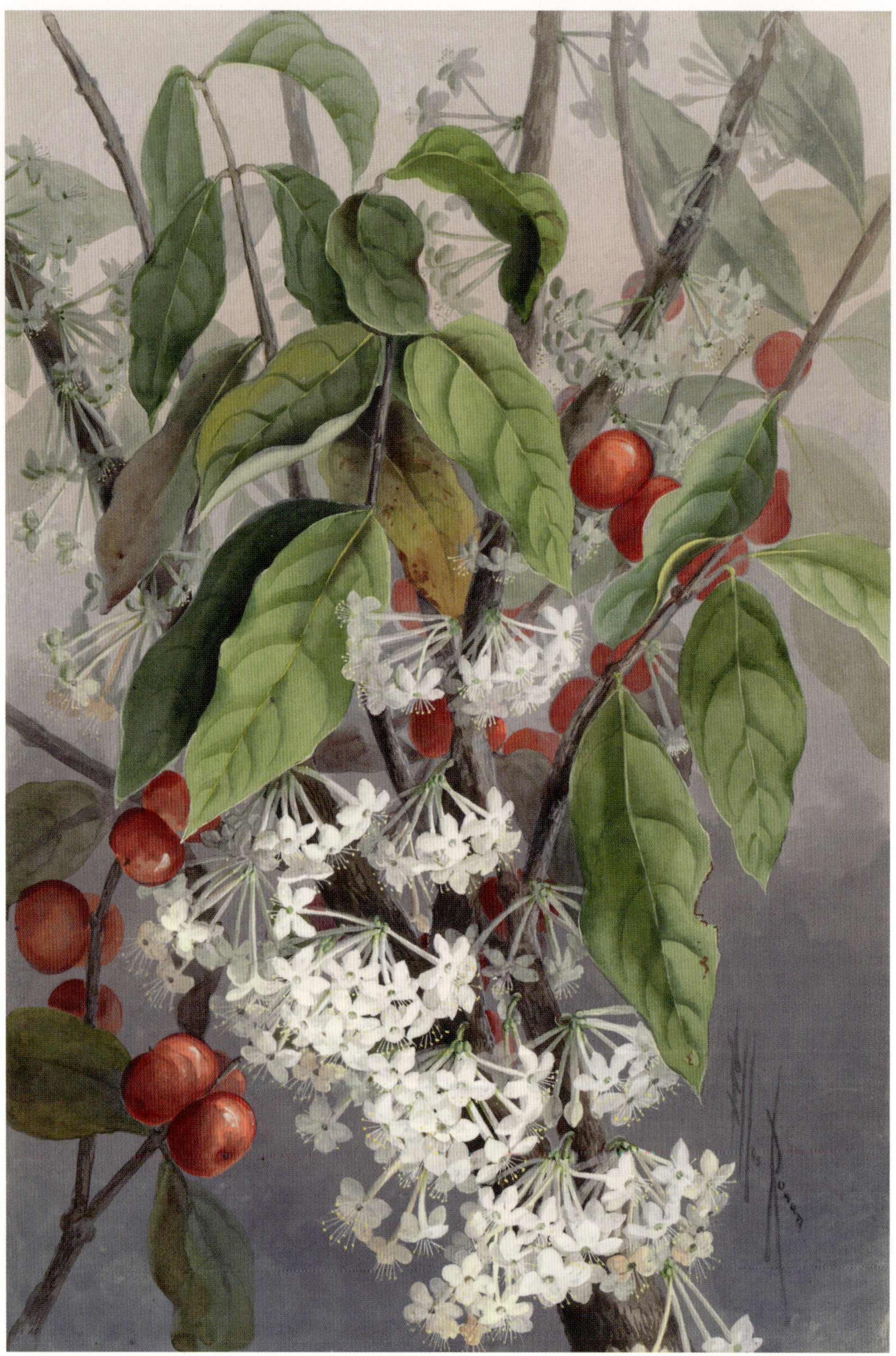

Phaleria Jack c.1911
gouache and watercolour on paper; 56.1 x 36.2 cm; Queensland
nla.cat-vn214524

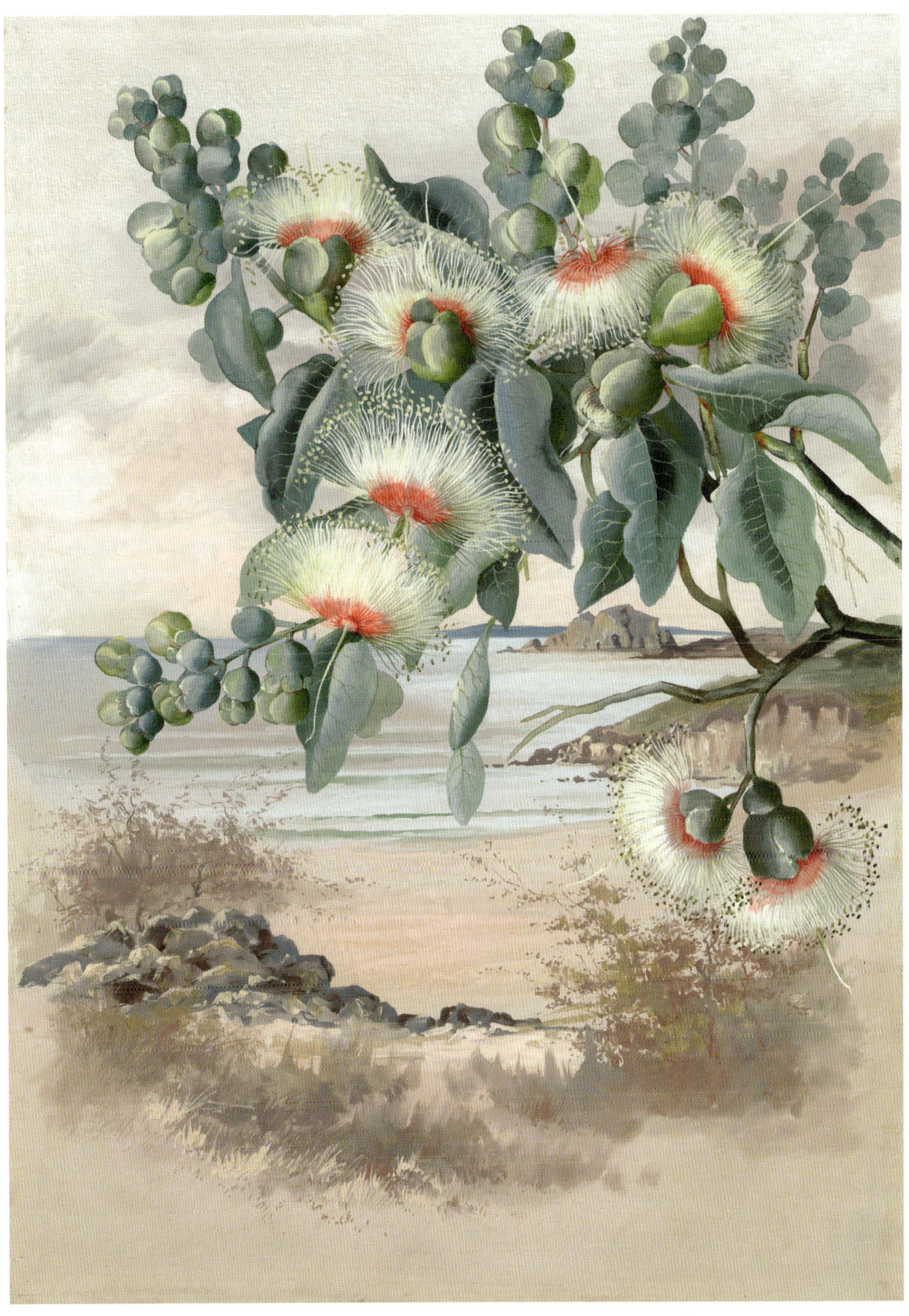

Cocky Apple Tree c.1911–1913
gouache and watercolour on paper; 55 x 38.5 cm; Dungeness, Herbert River, Queensland
nla.cat-vn1319342

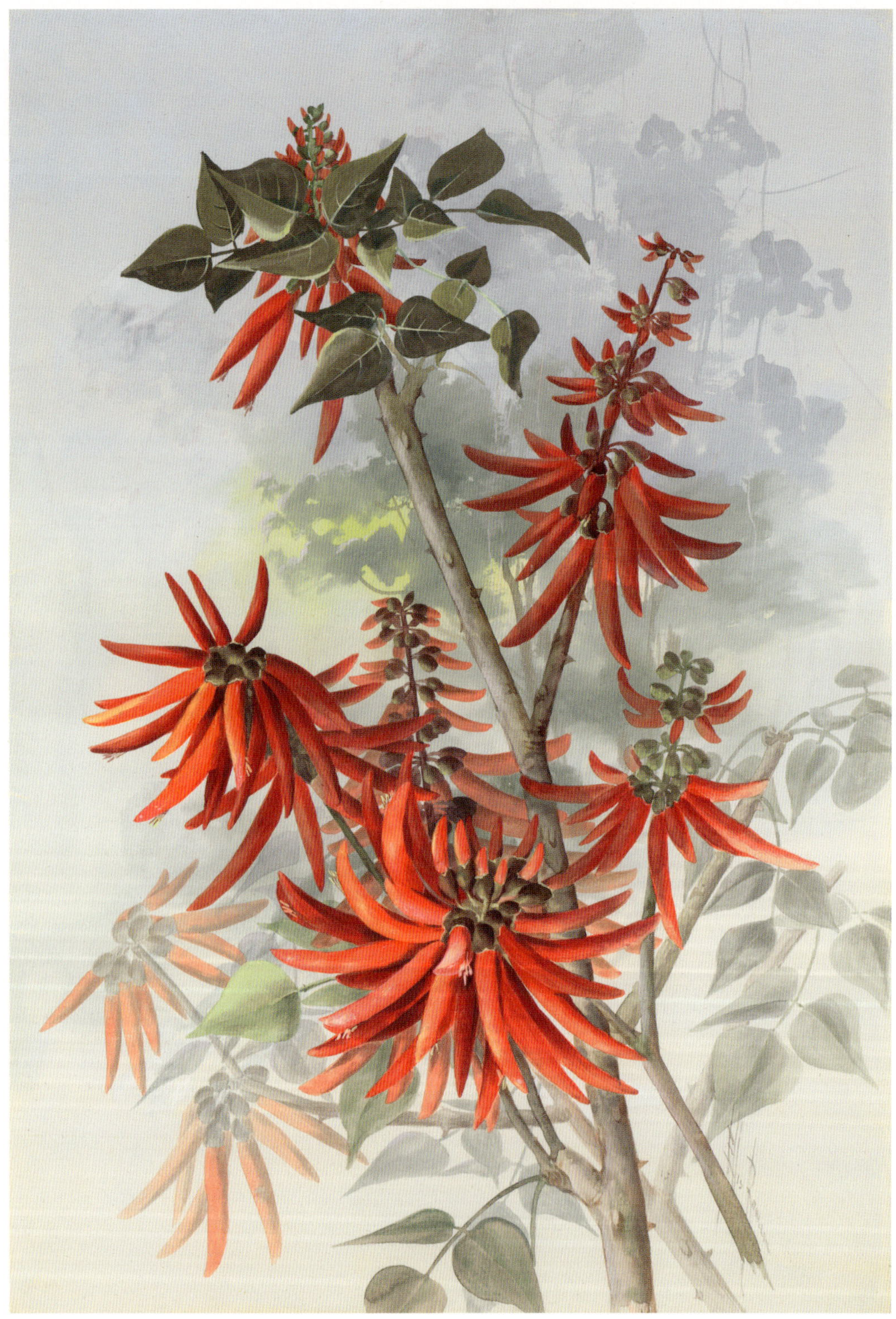

Coral Tree c.1911–1913
gouache and watercolour on paper; 54.7 x 38 cm; Queensland
nla.cat-vn2842558

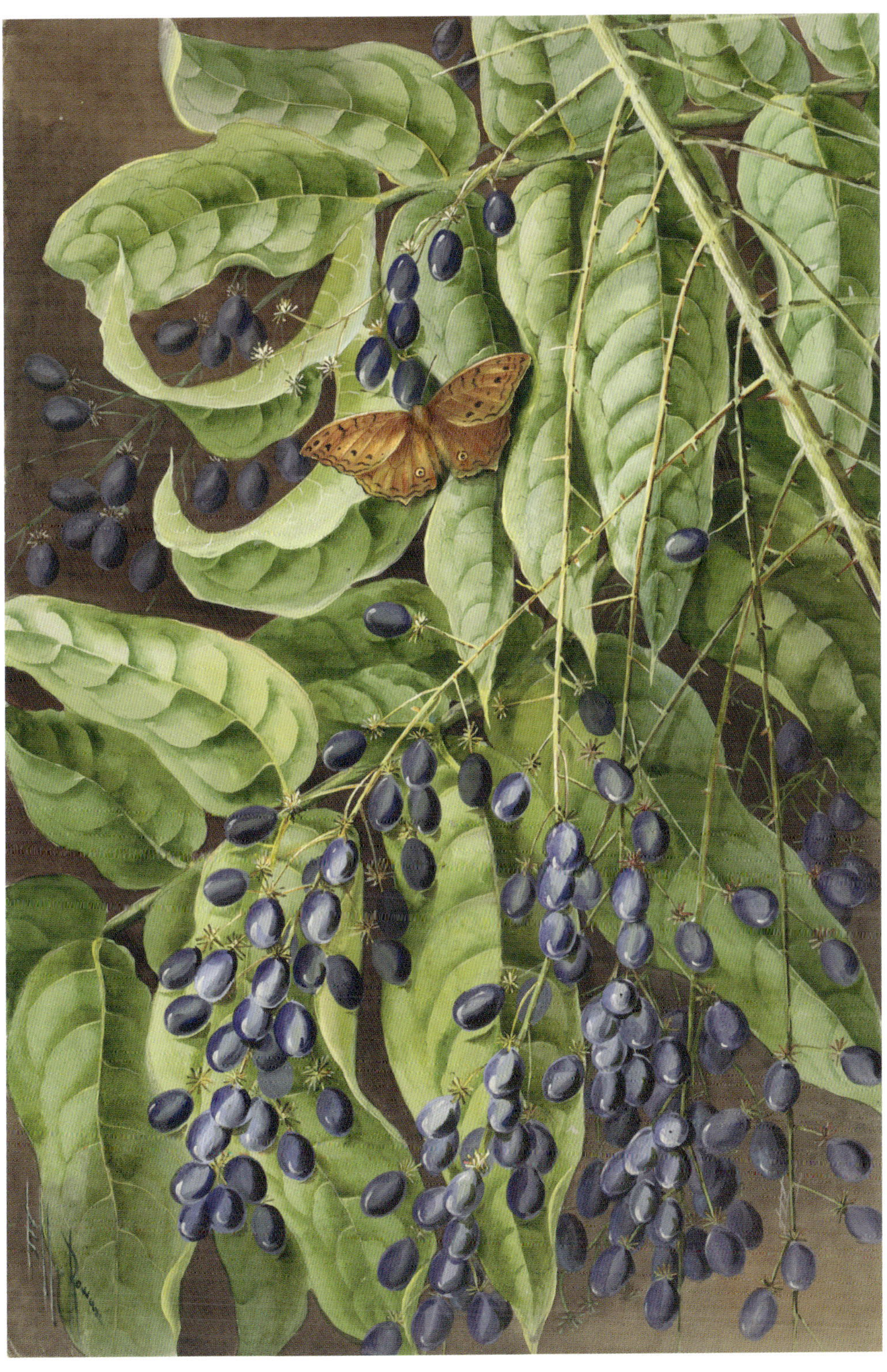

Blue Nun c.1911–1913
gouache and watercolour on paper; 56 x 38 cm; Queensland
nla.cat-vn2845220

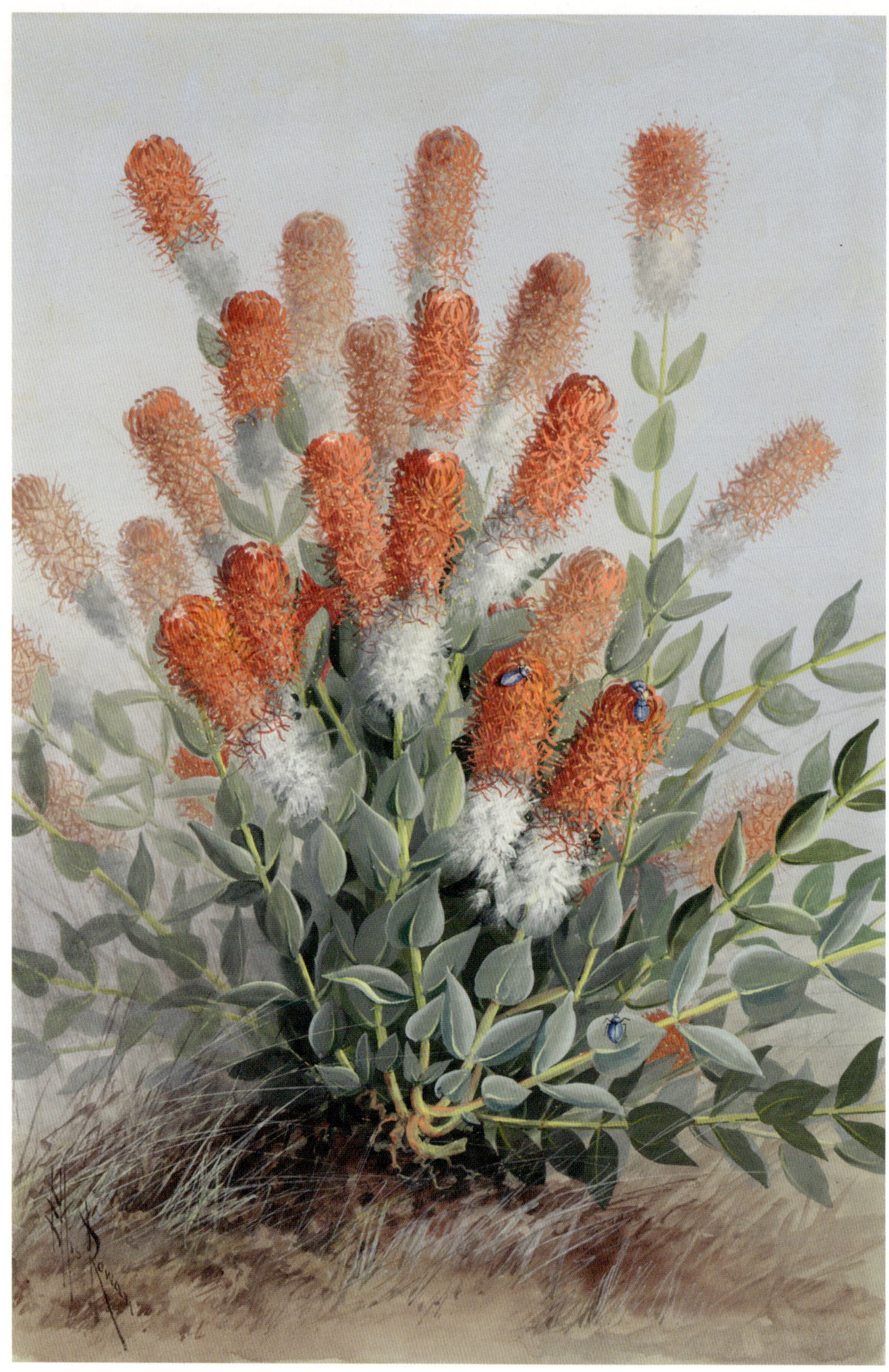

Flinders Poppy c.1911–1913
gouache and watercolour on paper; 56 x 38 cm; Queensland
nla.cat-vn1320081

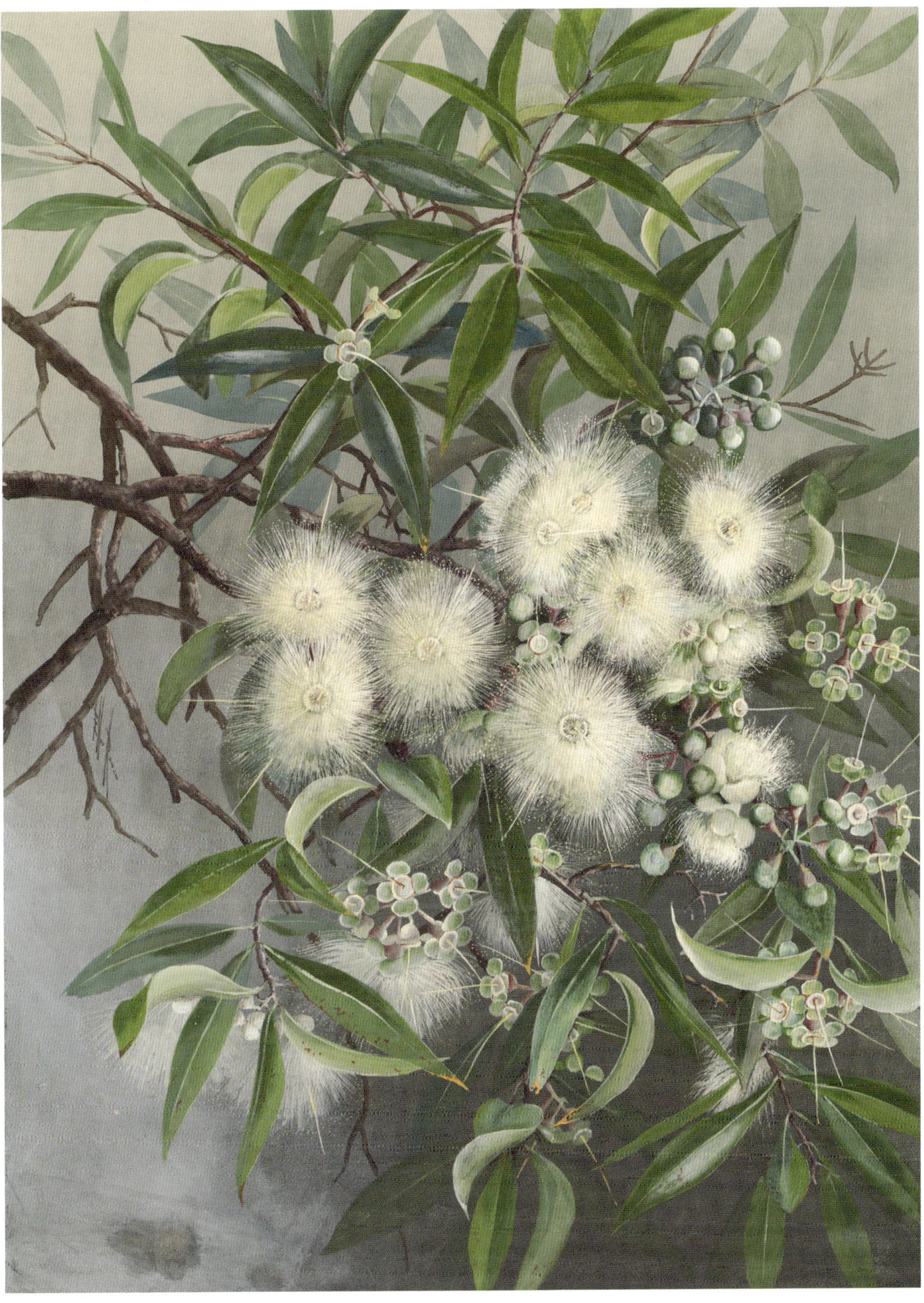

River Cherry c.1911–1913
gouache and watercolour on paper; 75 x 56.3 cm; Queensland
nla.cat-vn226311

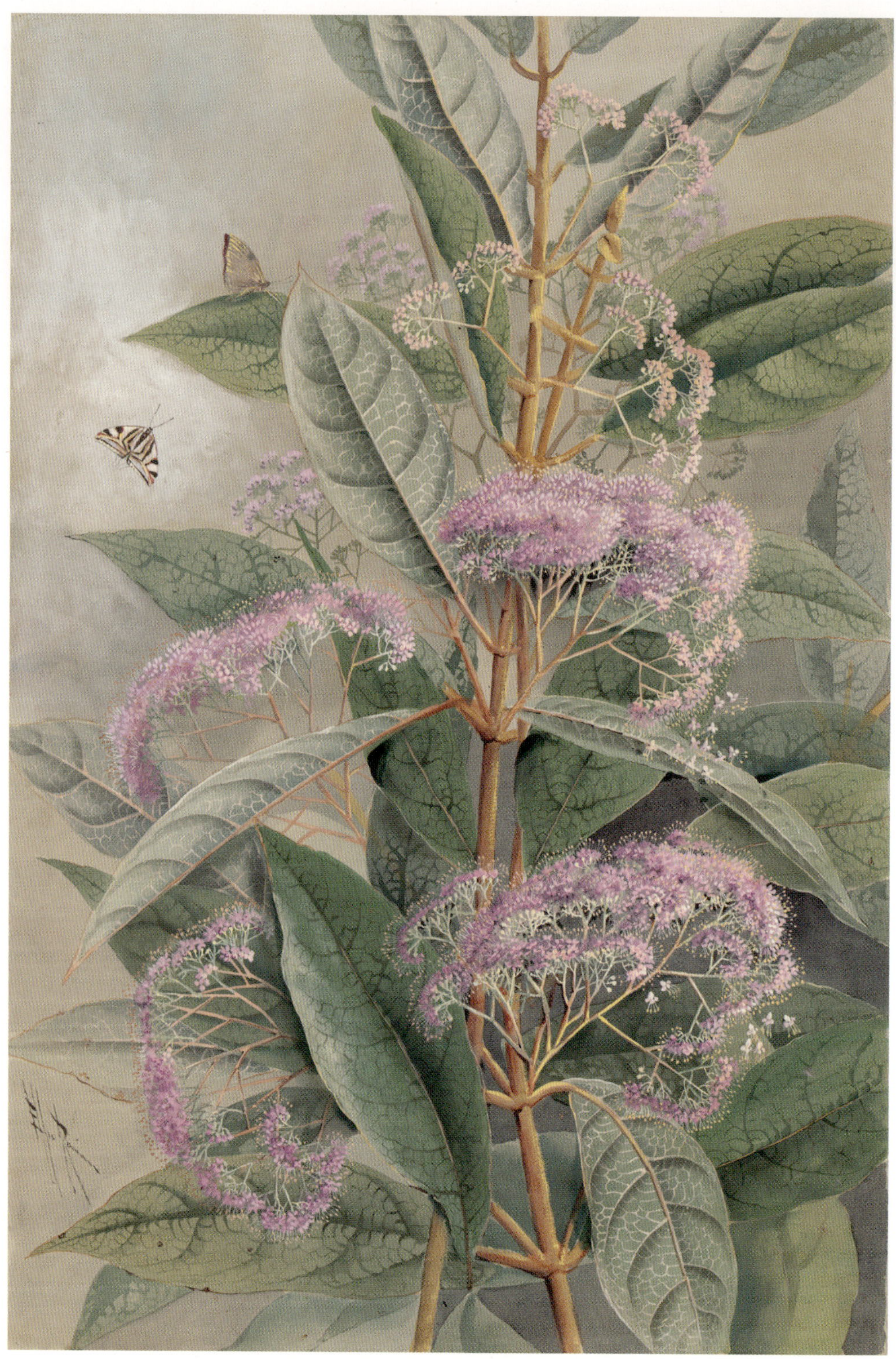

Velvet Leaf c.1916
gouache and watercolour on paper; 56 x 38 cm; Papua New Guinea
nla.cat-vn2691298

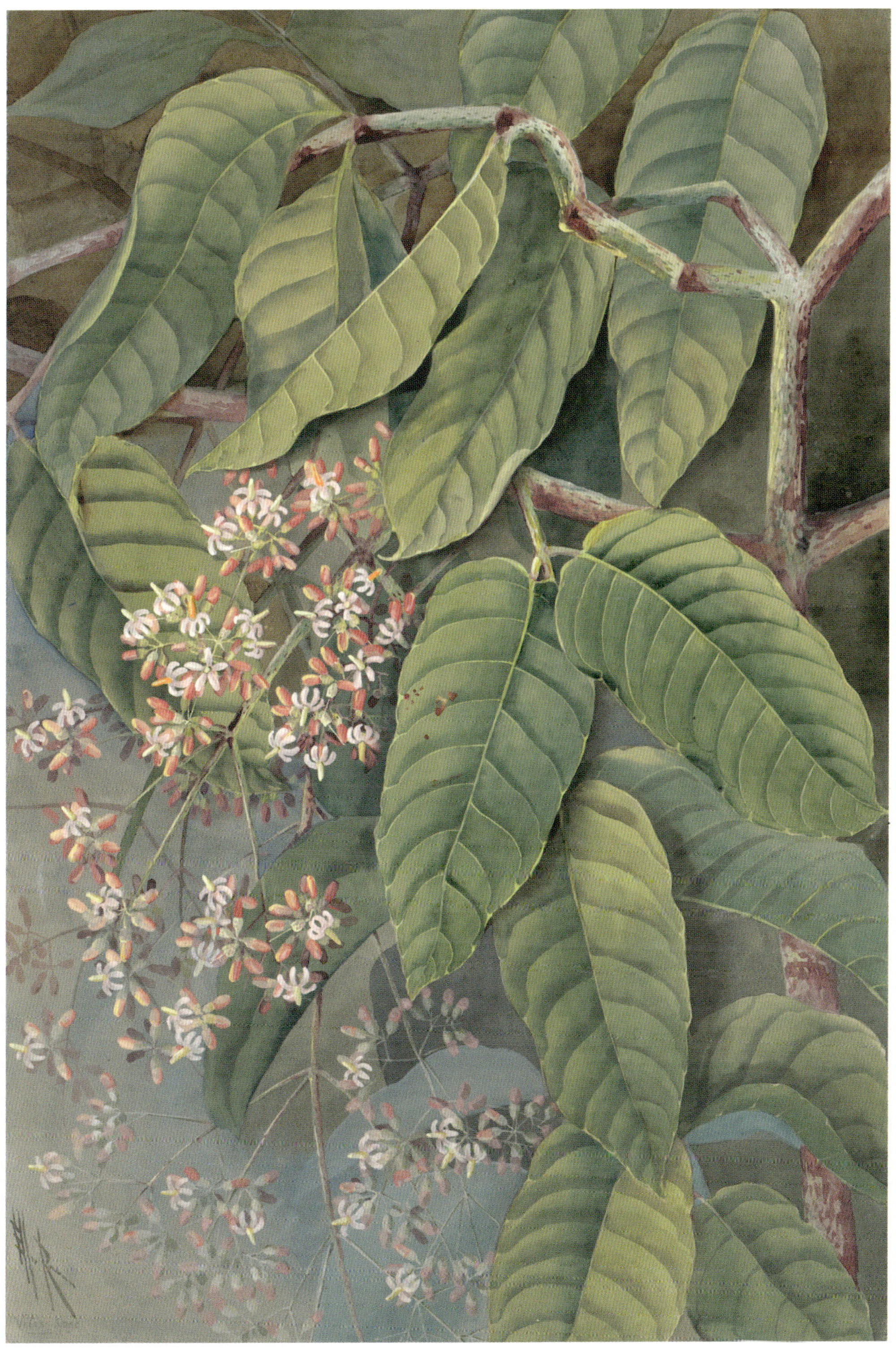

Green Plum c.1916
gouache and watercolour on paper; 56 x 38 cm
nla.cat-vn2689643

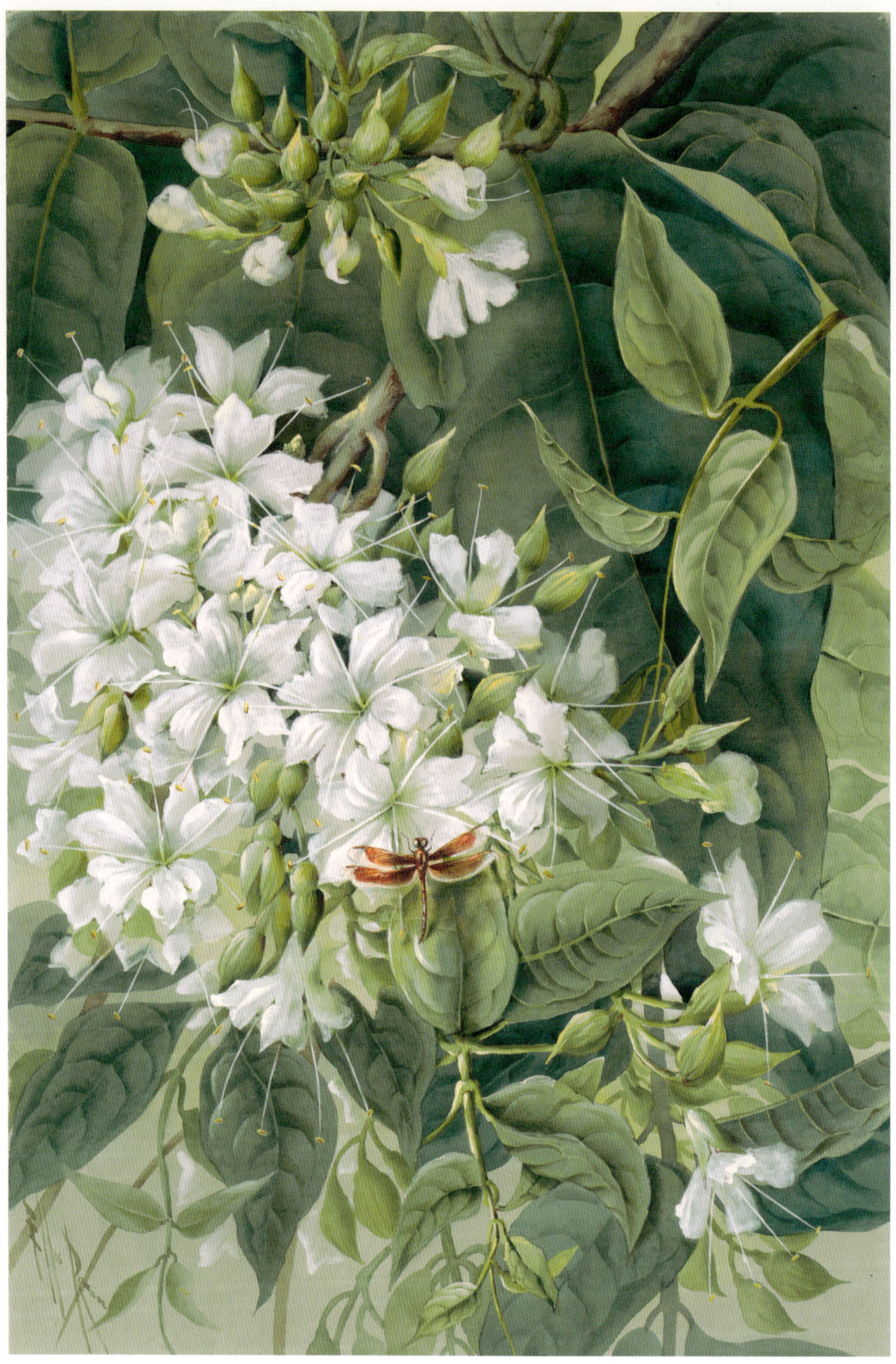

October Glory c.1916
gouache and watercolour on paper; 56 x 38 cm; Papua New Guinea
nla.cat-vn1168516

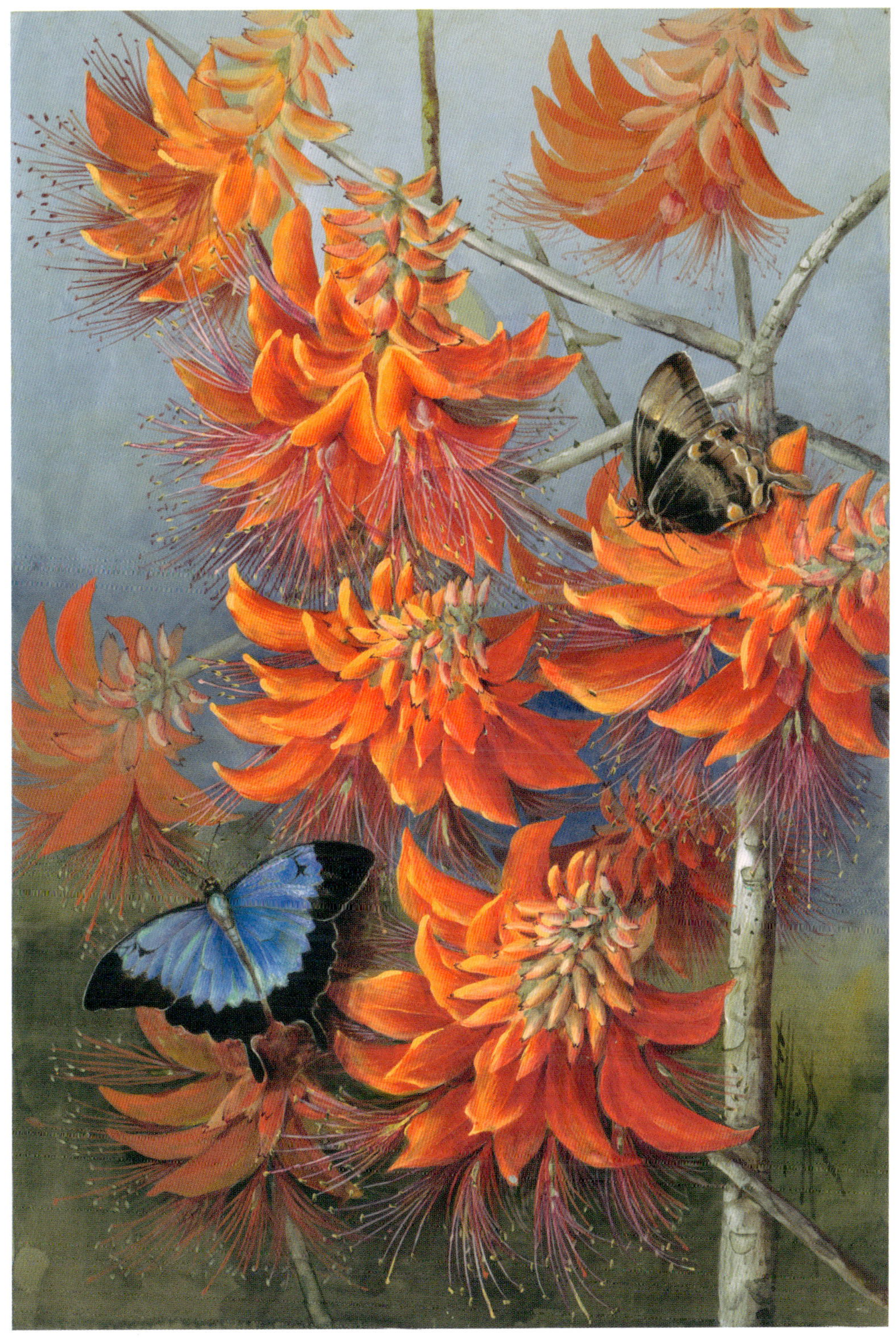

Coral Tree c.1916
gouache and watercolour on paper, 55.5 x 38 cm; Papua New Guinea
nla.cat-vn1168540

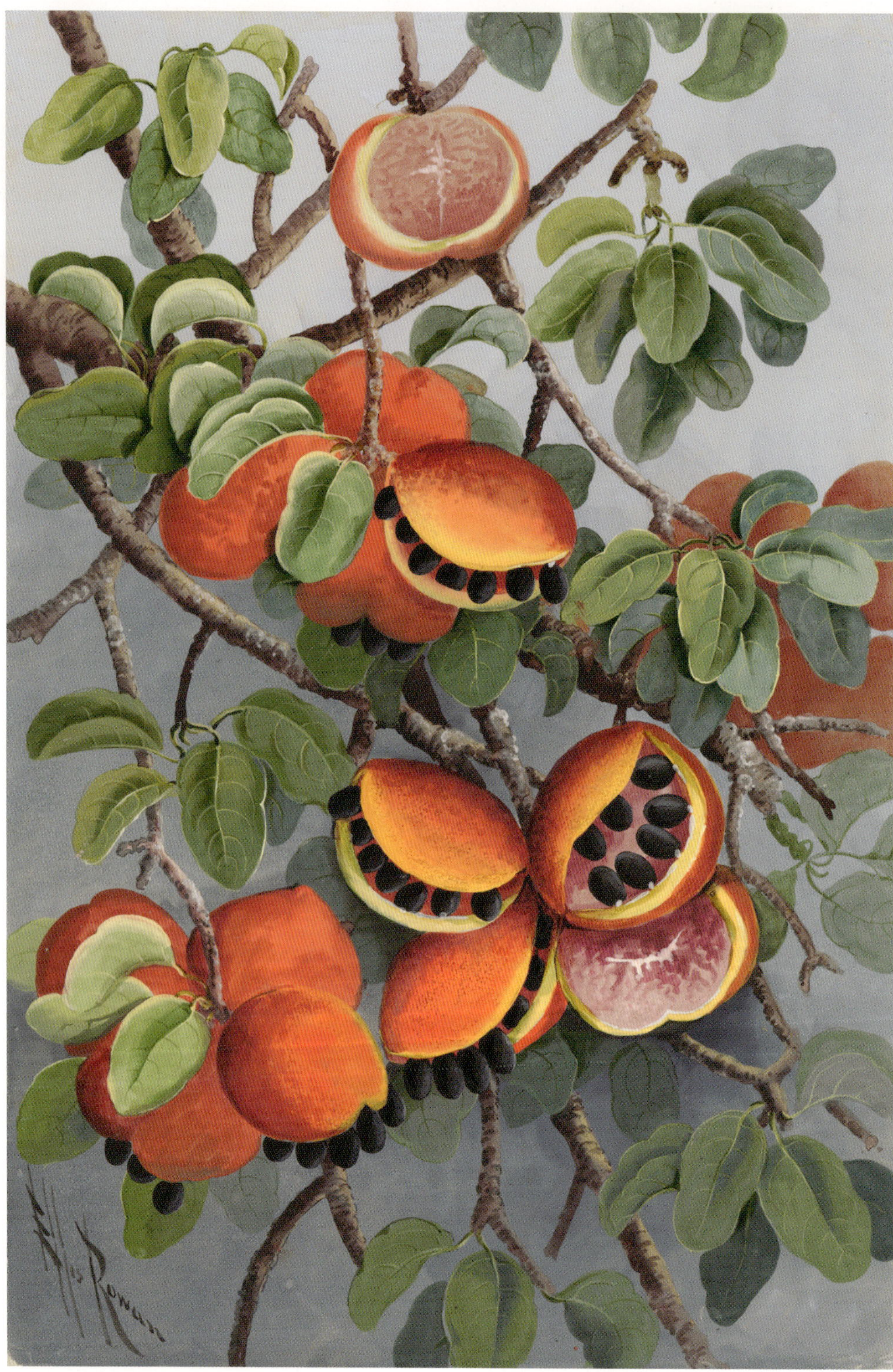

Orange Fruited Sterculia c.1916
gouache and watercolour on paper; 56 x 38.2 cm; Papua New Guinea
nla.cat-vn2690796

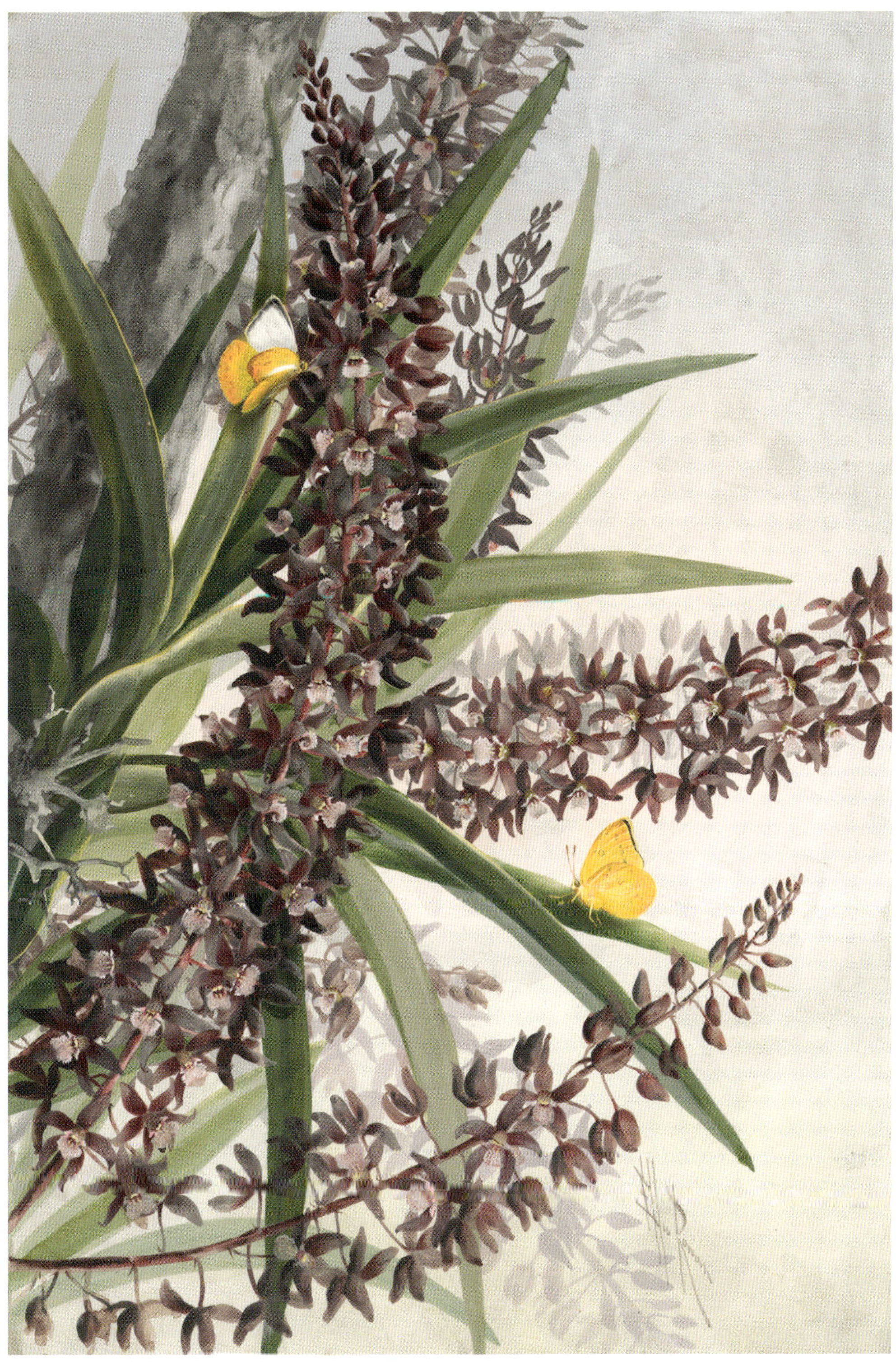

Tiger Orchid c.1916
gouache and watercolour on paper; 56 x 38 cm; Papua New Guinea
nla.cat-vn1168163

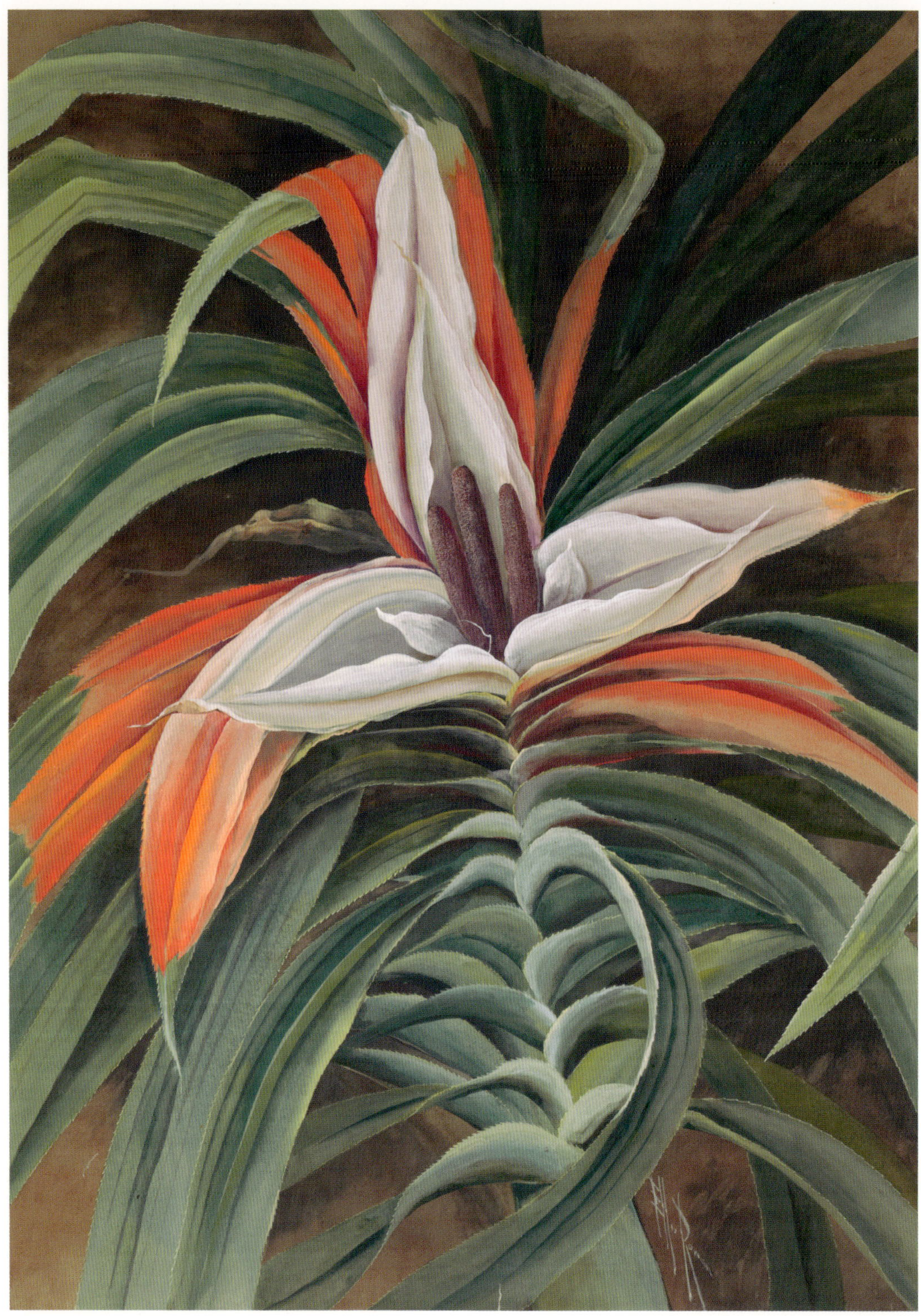

[*Freycinetia gaudich.*] c.1916
gouache and watercolour on paper; 75 x 54.6 cm; Papua New Guinea
nla.cat-vn1167932

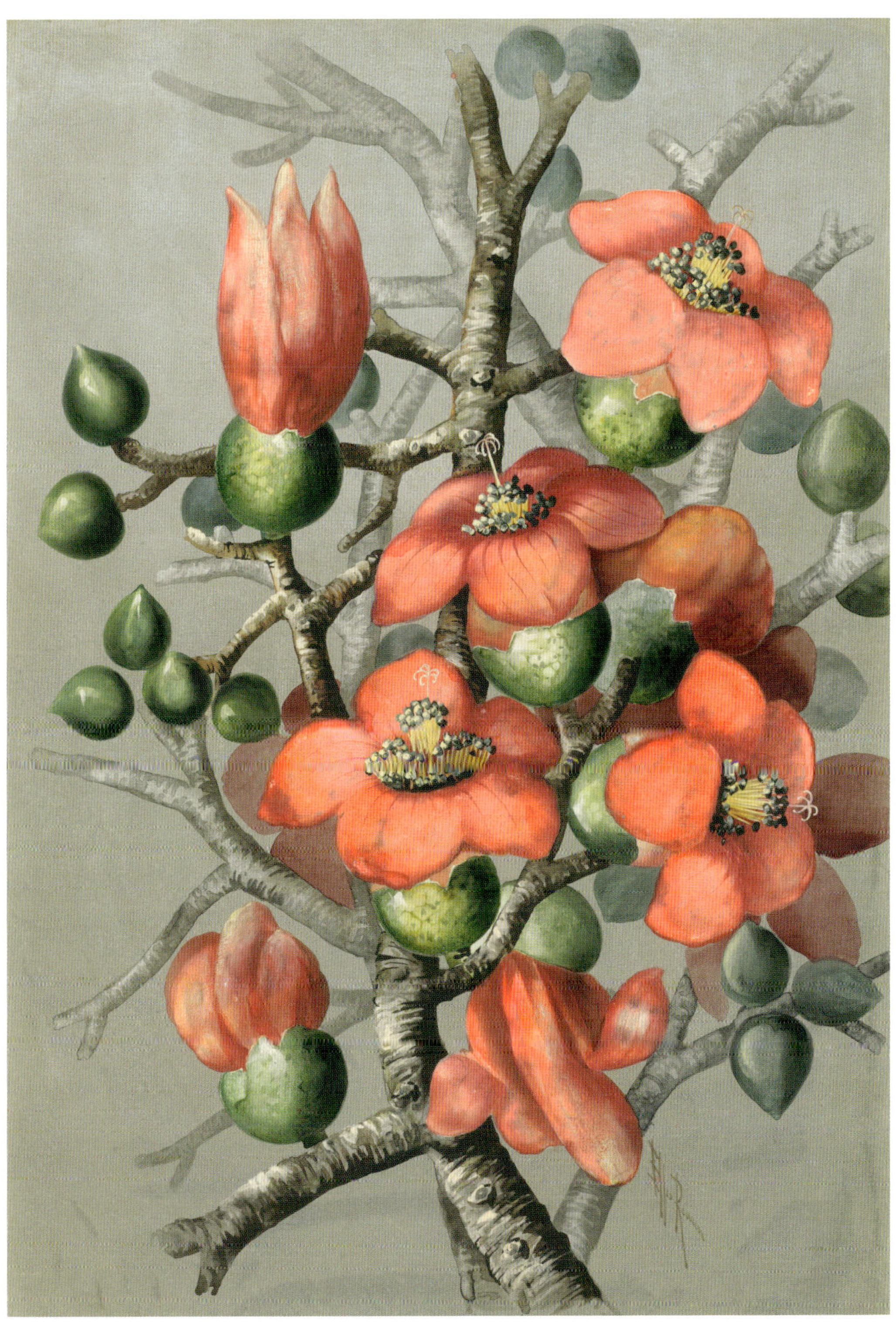

Silk Cotton Tree c.1916
gouache and watercolour on paper; 55 x 38 cm; Papua New Guinea
nla.cat-vn2688942

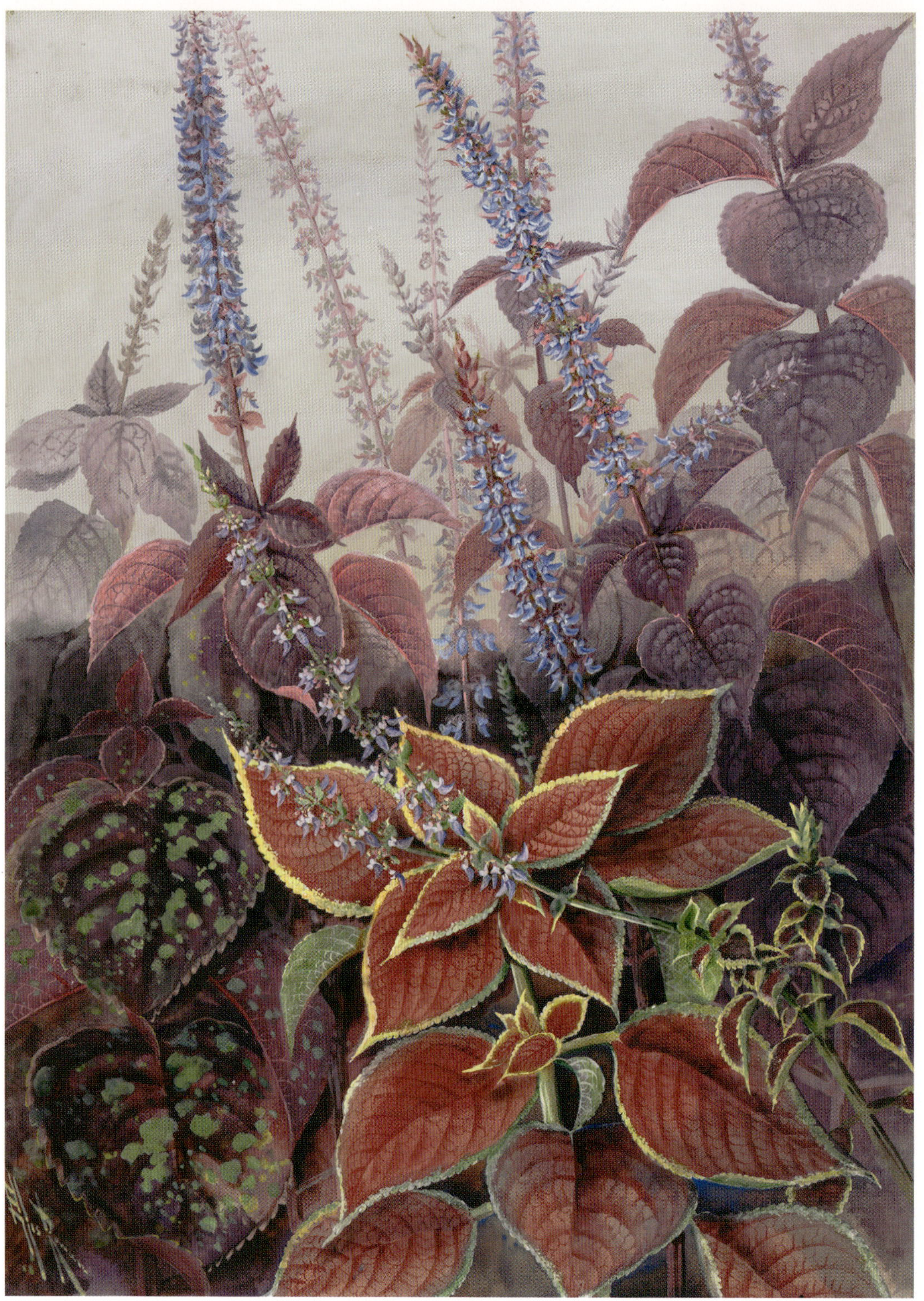

Painted Nettle c.1916
gouache and watercolour on paper; 76.3 x 56 cm; Papua New Guinea
nla.cat-vn1737366

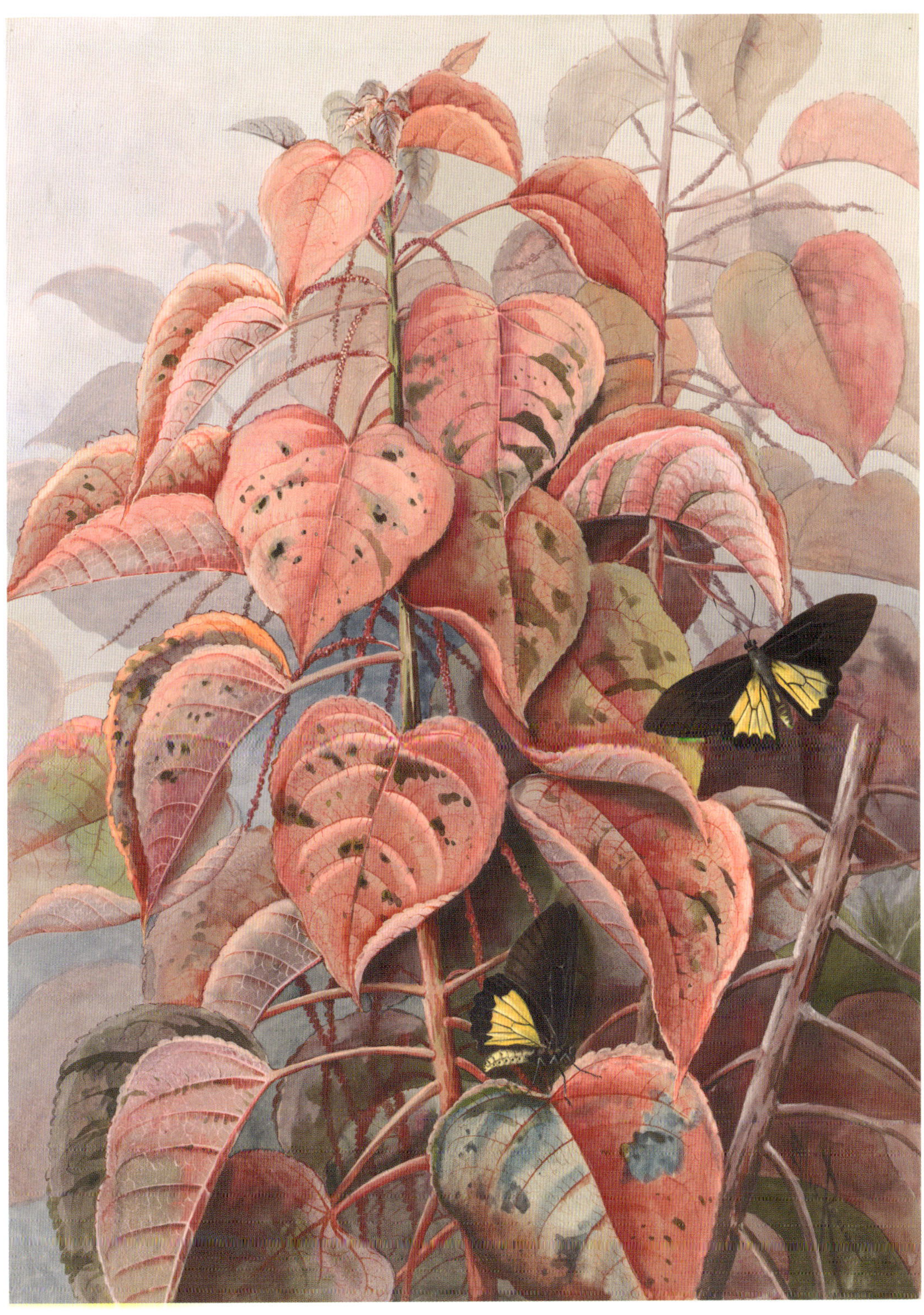

Birdwing Butterfly c.1916
gouache and watercolour on paper; 76 x 55.9 cm; Papua New Guinea
nla.cat-vn1748741

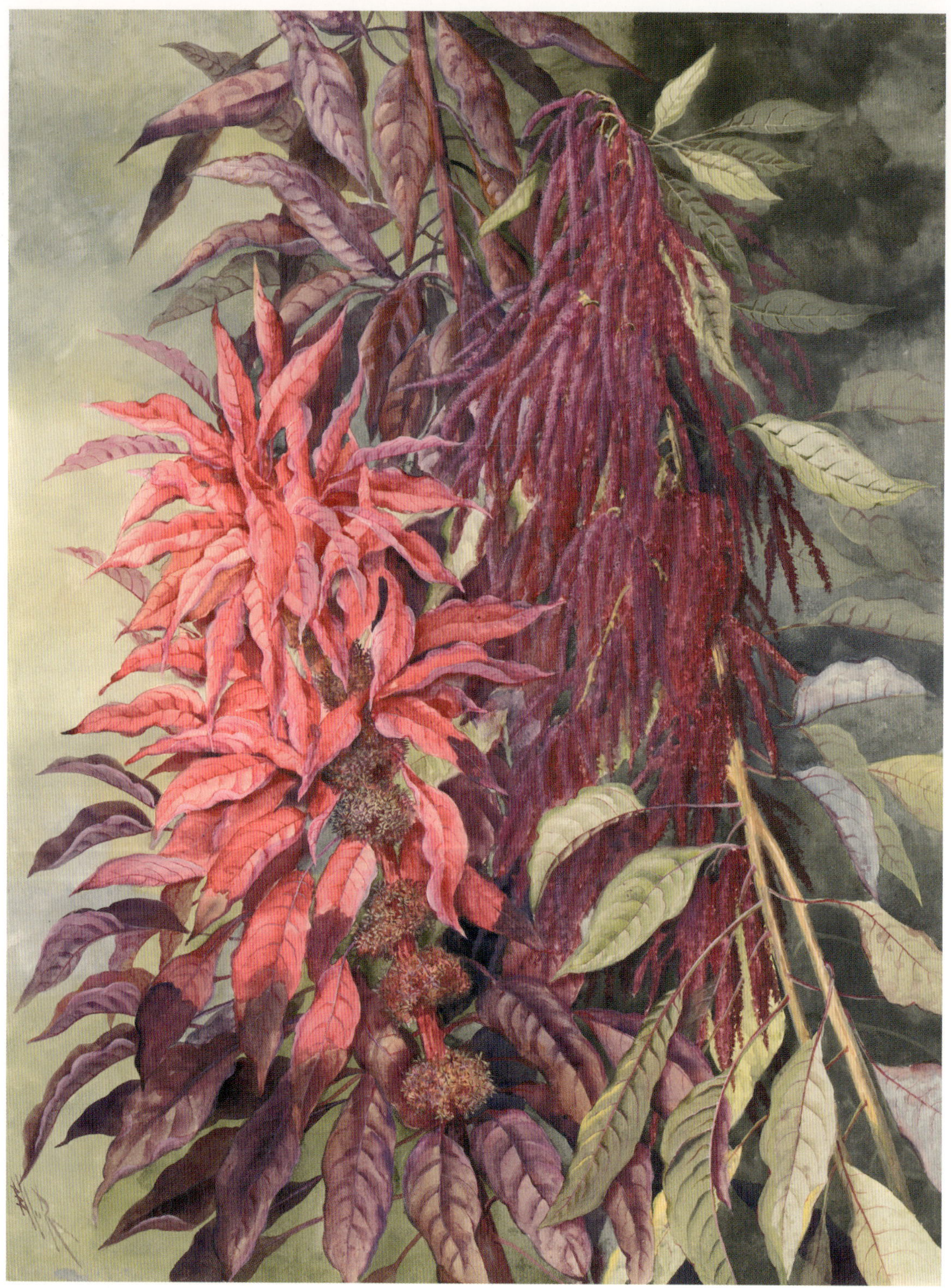

Tassel Flower c.1916
gouache and watercolour on paper; 78.5 x 60.2 cm; Papua New Guinea
nla.cat-vn226292

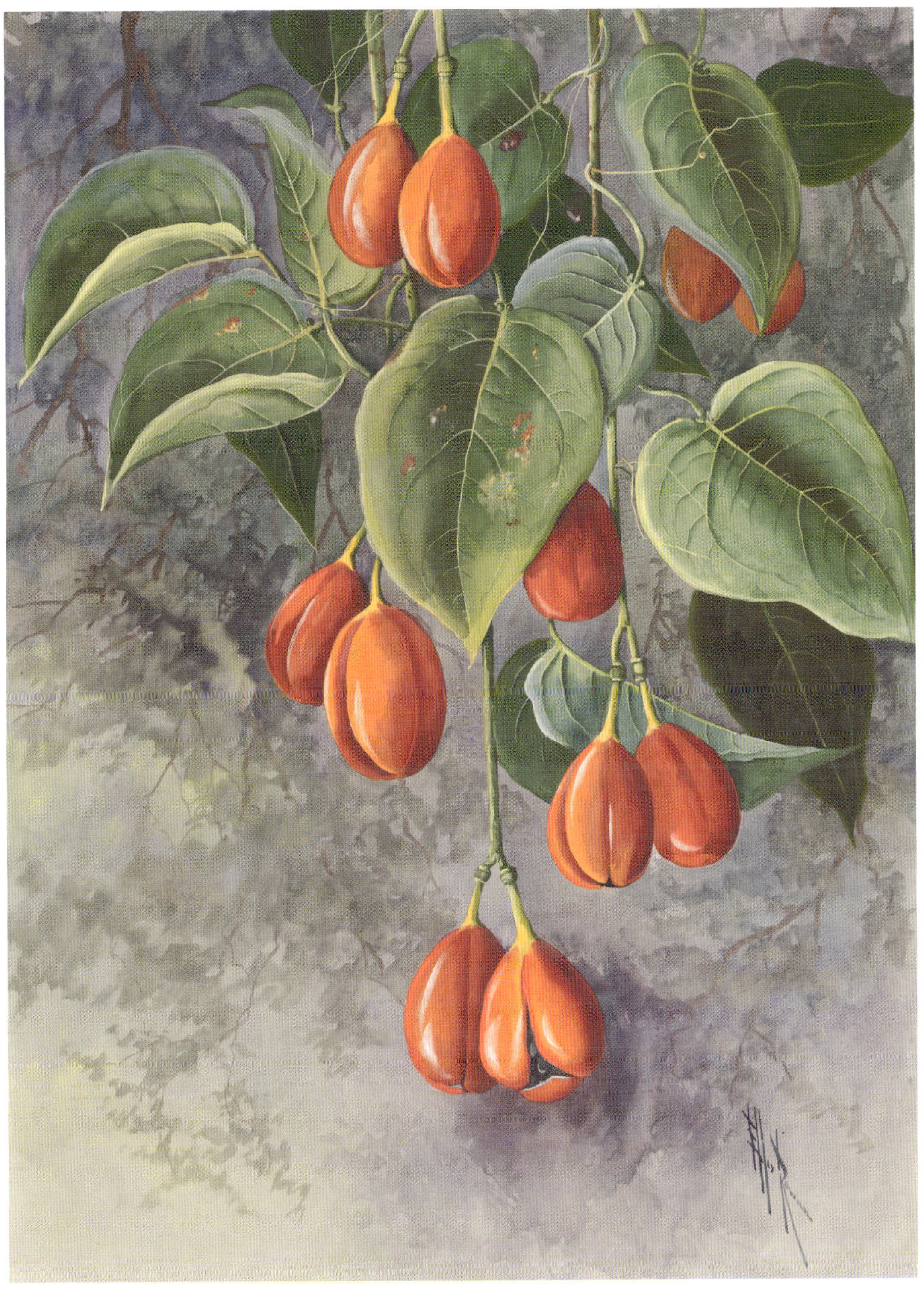

Lacewing Vine, c.1916
gouache and watercolour on paper; 75.8 x 56 cm; Papua New Guinea
nla.cat-vn1736997

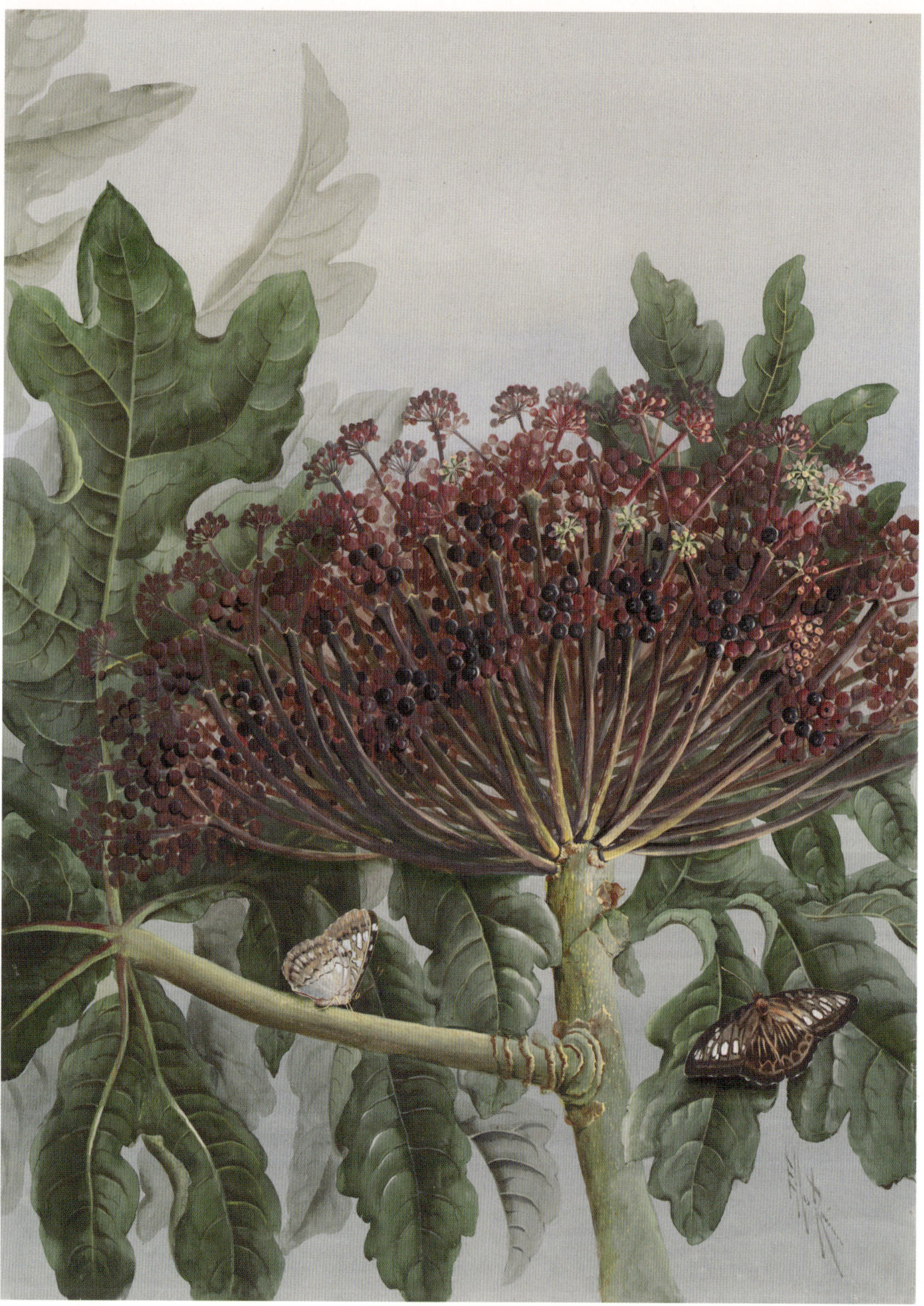

Miagos Bush c.1916
gouache and watercolour on paper; 76.1 x 55.8 cm; Papua New Guinea
nla.cat-vn214544

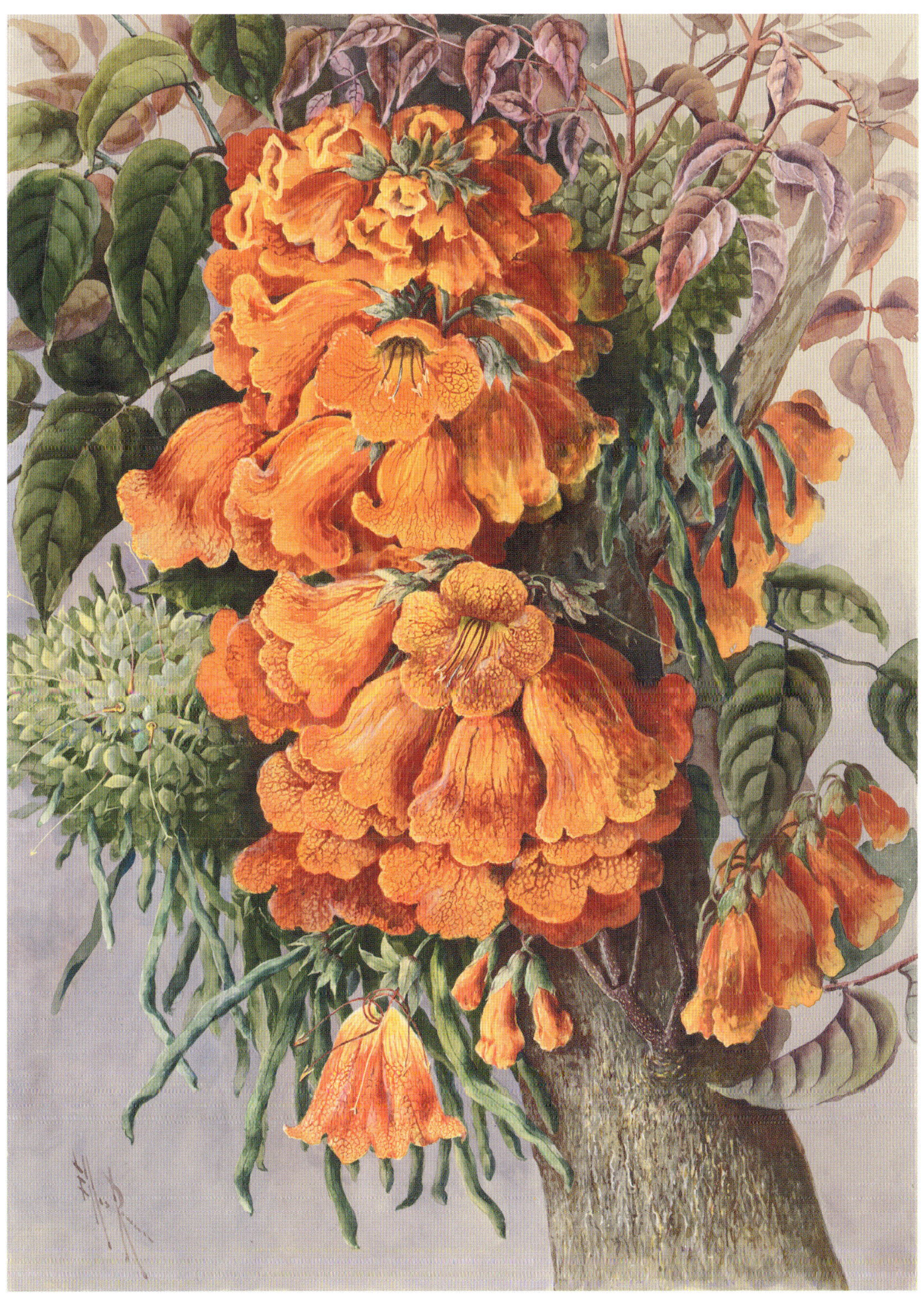

[Lamiodendron magnificum] c 1916
gouache and watercolour on paper; 75.9 x 55.9 cm; Papua New Guinea
nla.cat-vn1748721

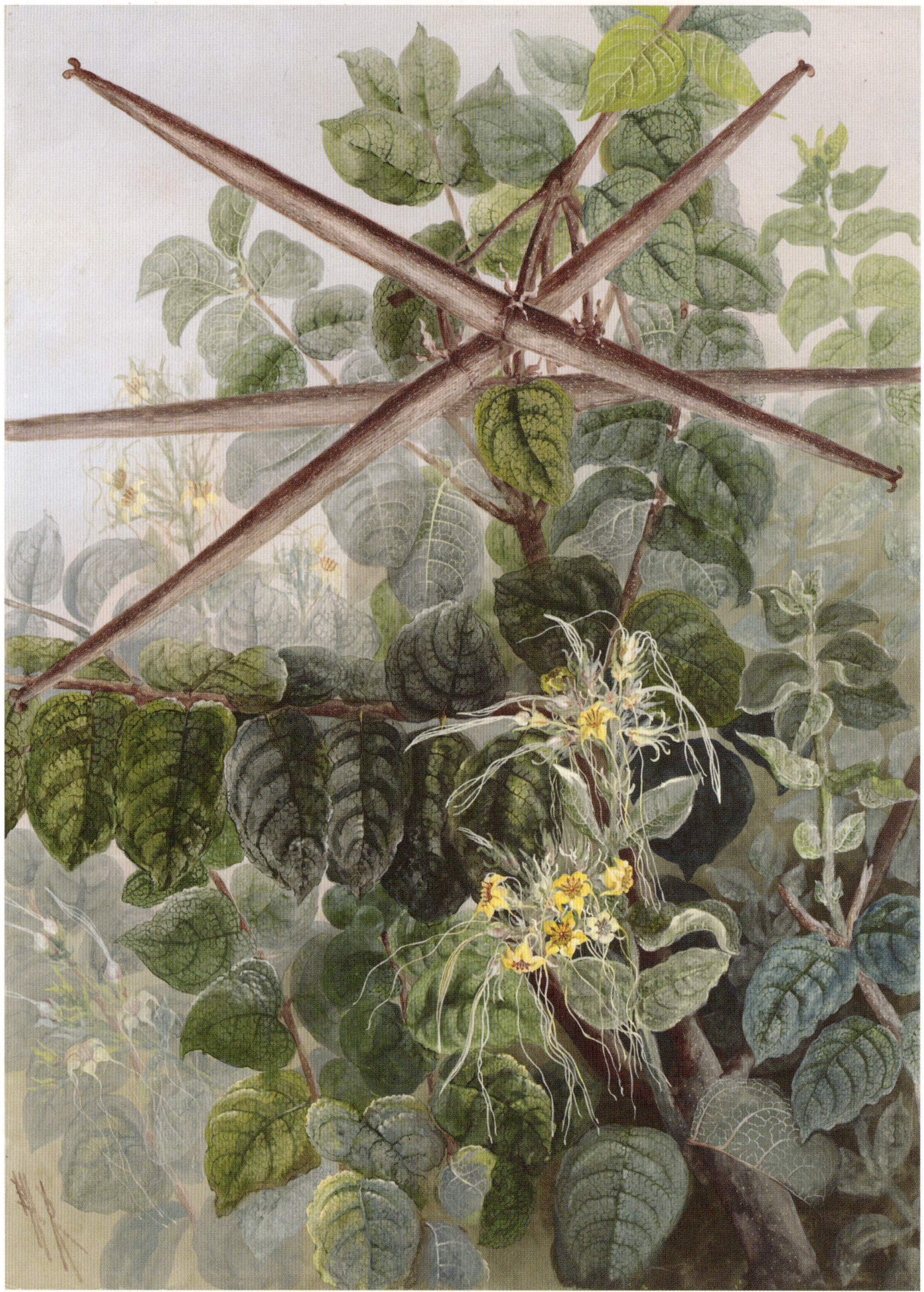

Leaves and Flowers of Plant from Papua New Guinea c.1916
gouache and watercolour on paper; 76 x 56 cm; Papua New Guinea
nla.cat-vn212435

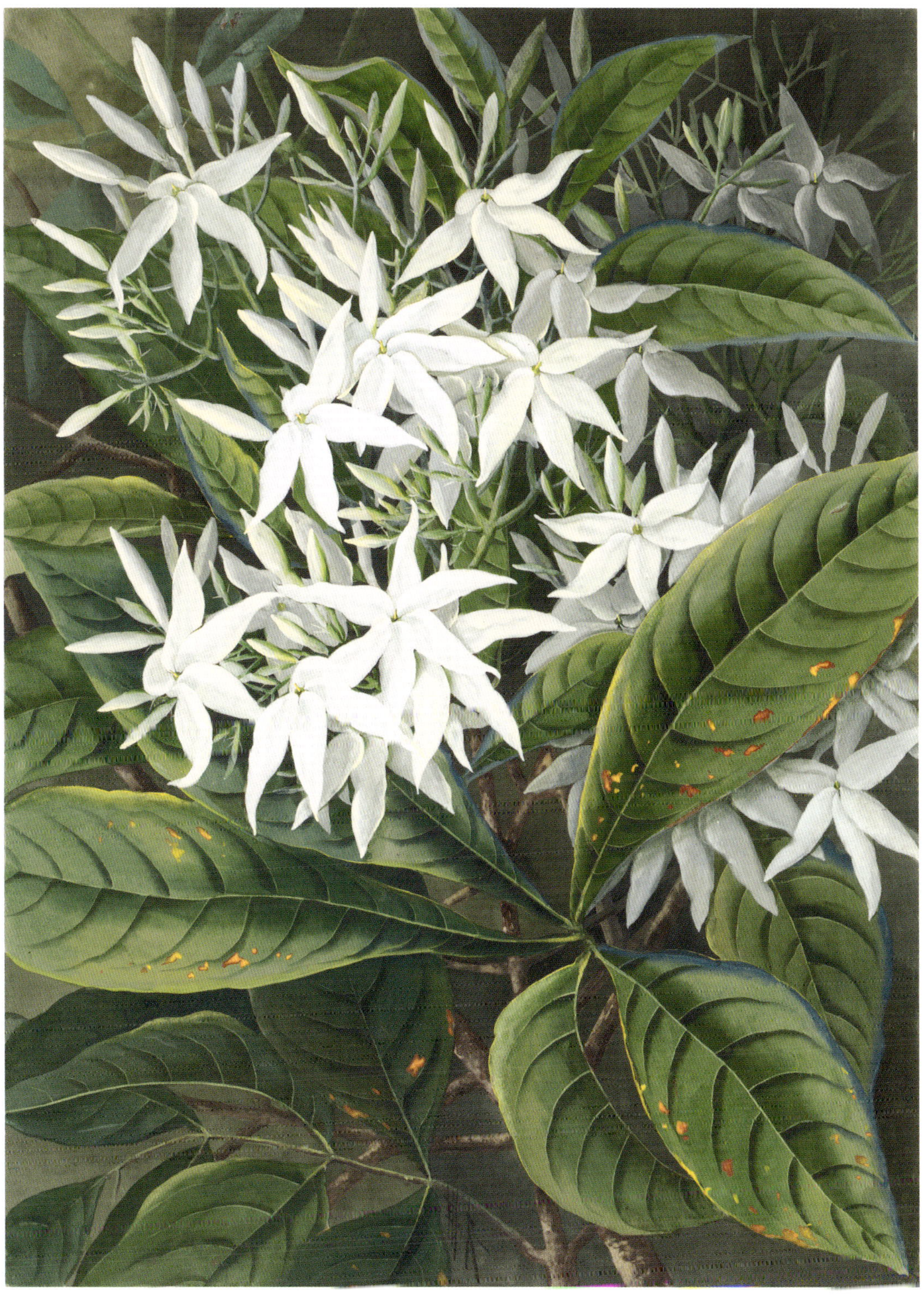

Native Gardenia, c.1916
gouache and watercolour on paper; 76.2 x 56 cm; Papua New Guinea
nla.cat-vn1748731

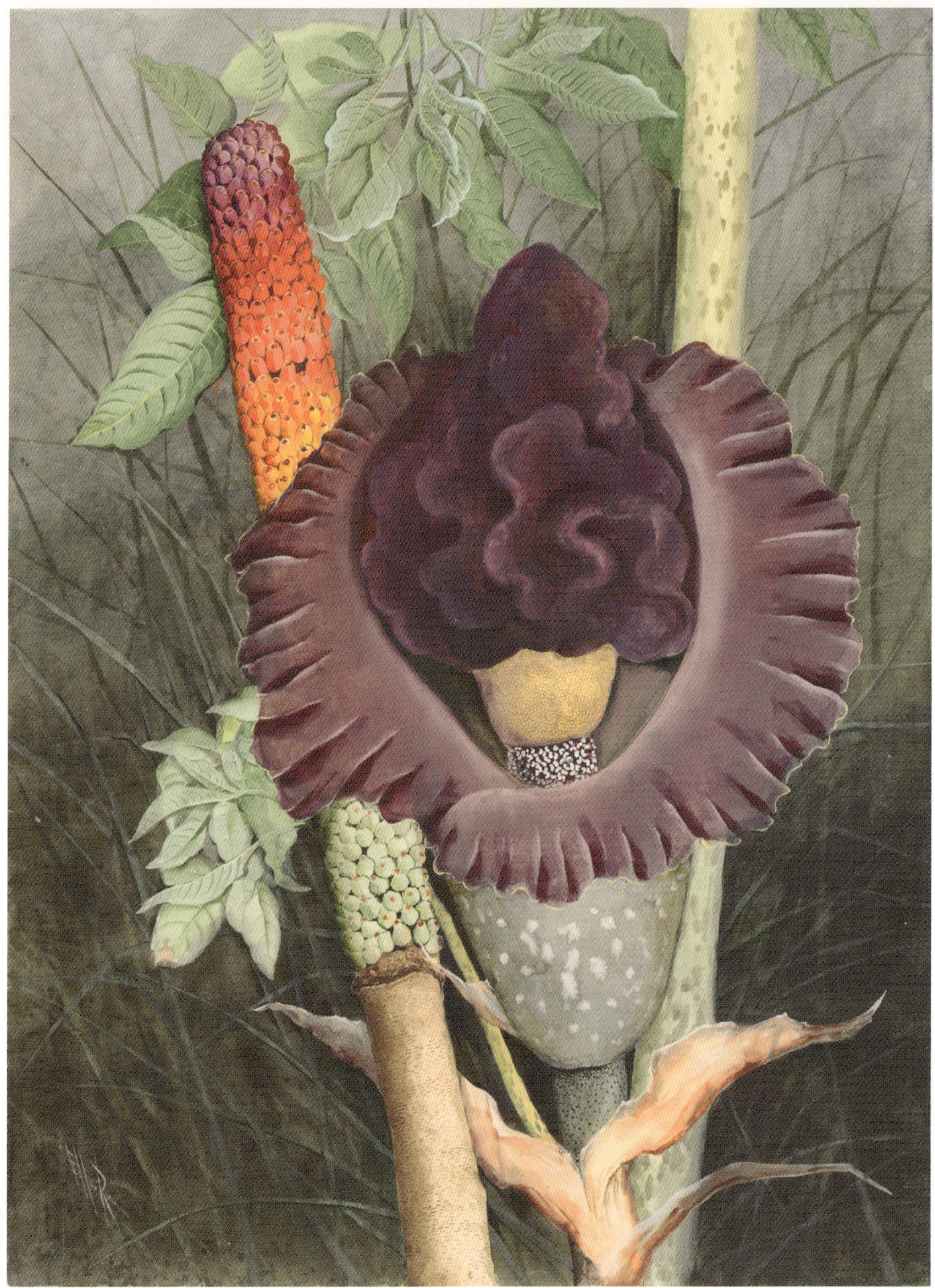

Elephant Plant c.1916
gouache and watercolour on paper; 78.3 x 58.7 cm; Papua New Guinea
nla.cat-vn2690063

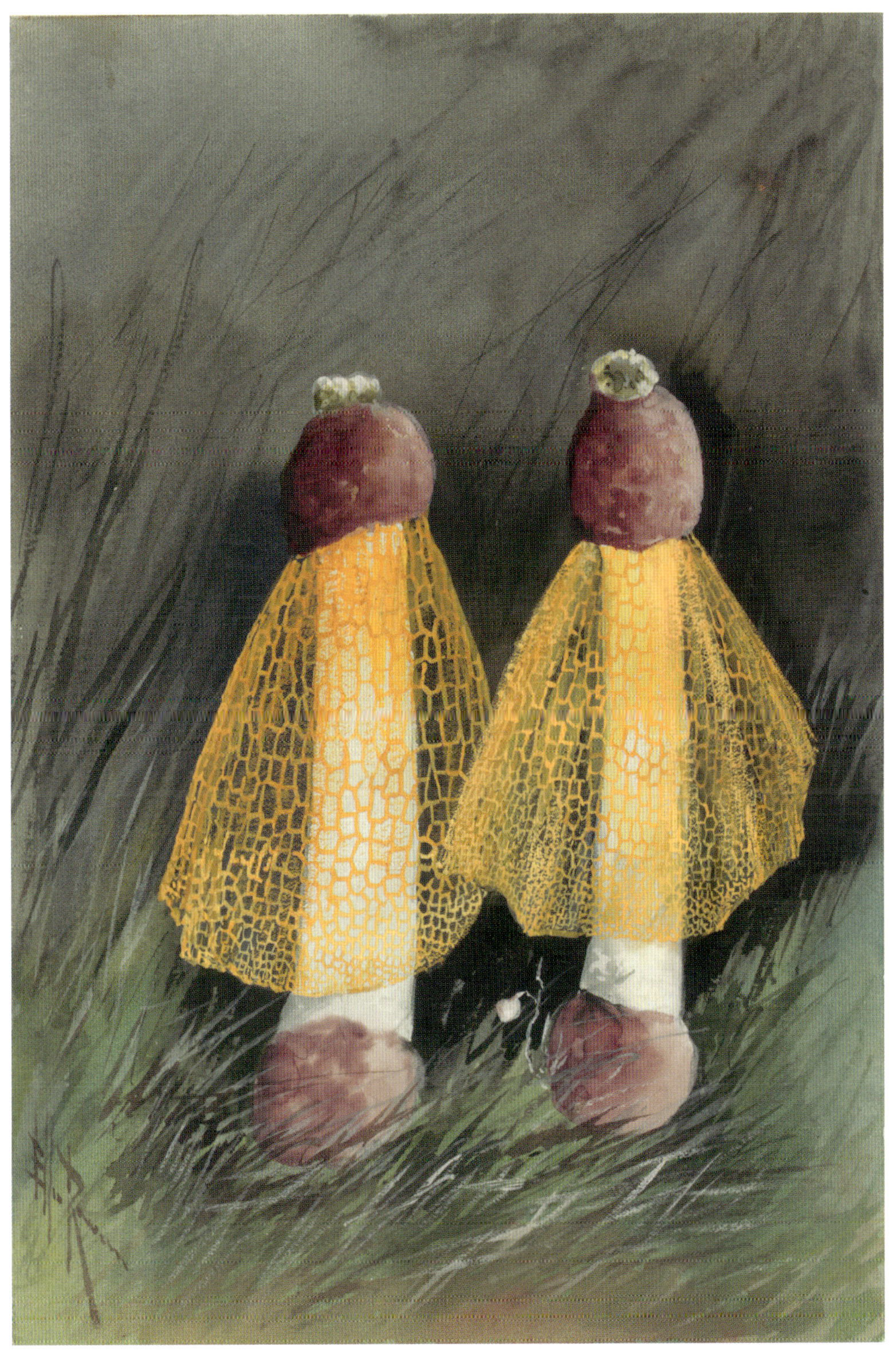

Netted Stinkhorn Fungus c.1916
gouache and watercolour on paper; 28 x 19 cm; Papua New Guinea
nla.cat-vn3292164

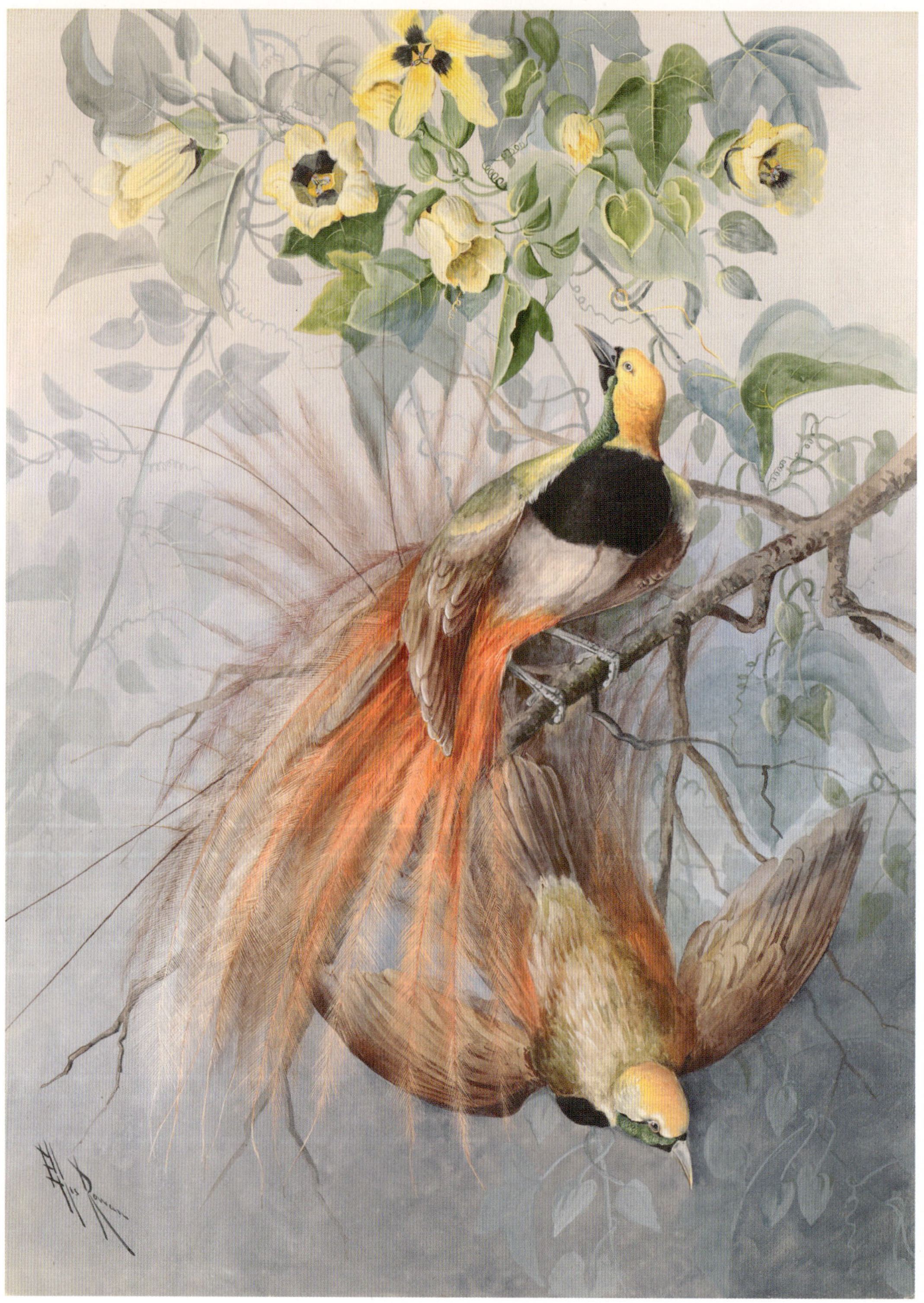

Count Raggi's Bird of Paradise c.1917
gouache and watercolour on paper; 76 x 56 cm; Papua New Guinea
nla.cat-vn2687189

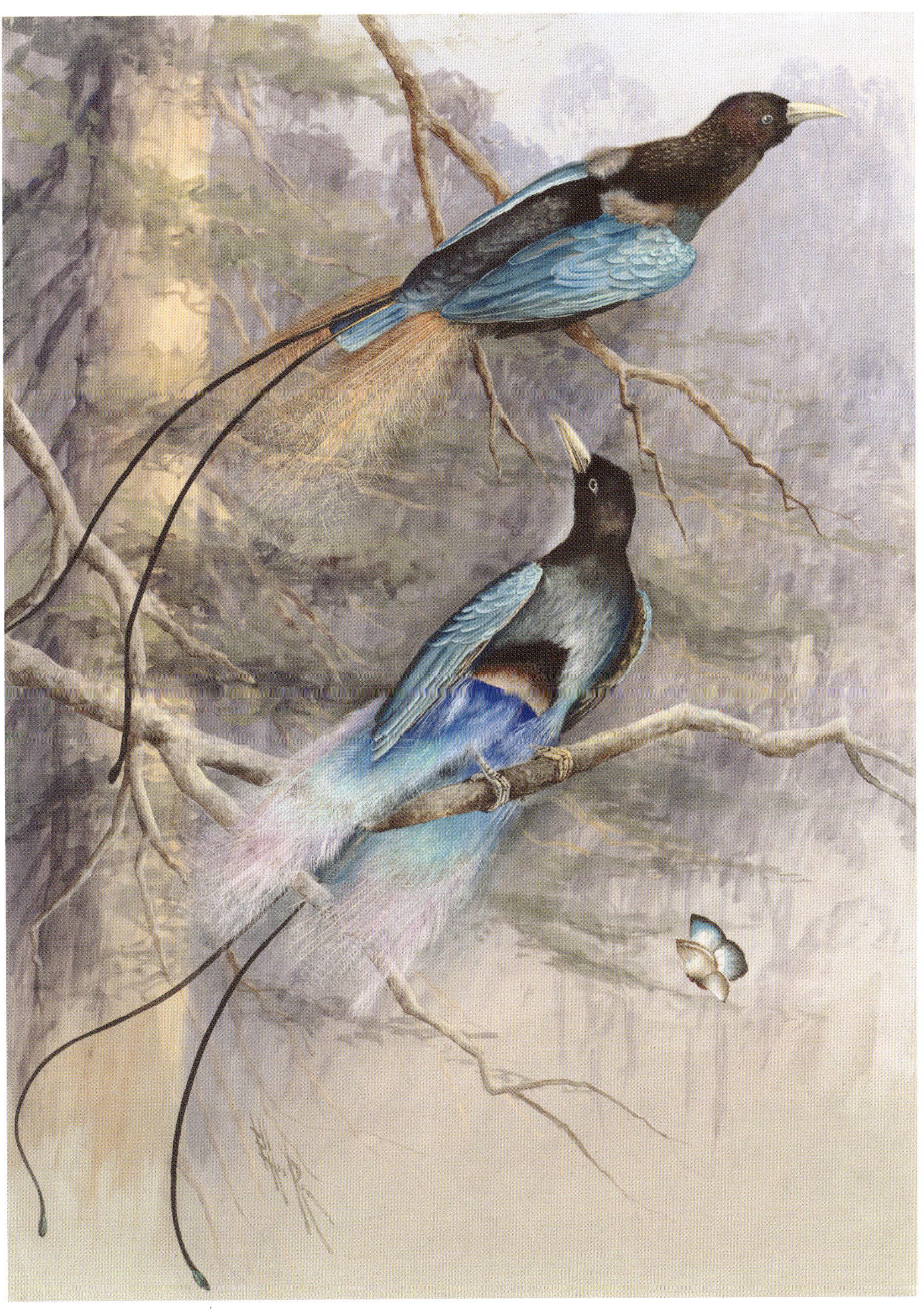

Elliot's Bird of Paradise c.1917
gouache and watercolour on paper; 76.1 x 55.5 cm; Papua New Guinea
nla.cat-vn2686637

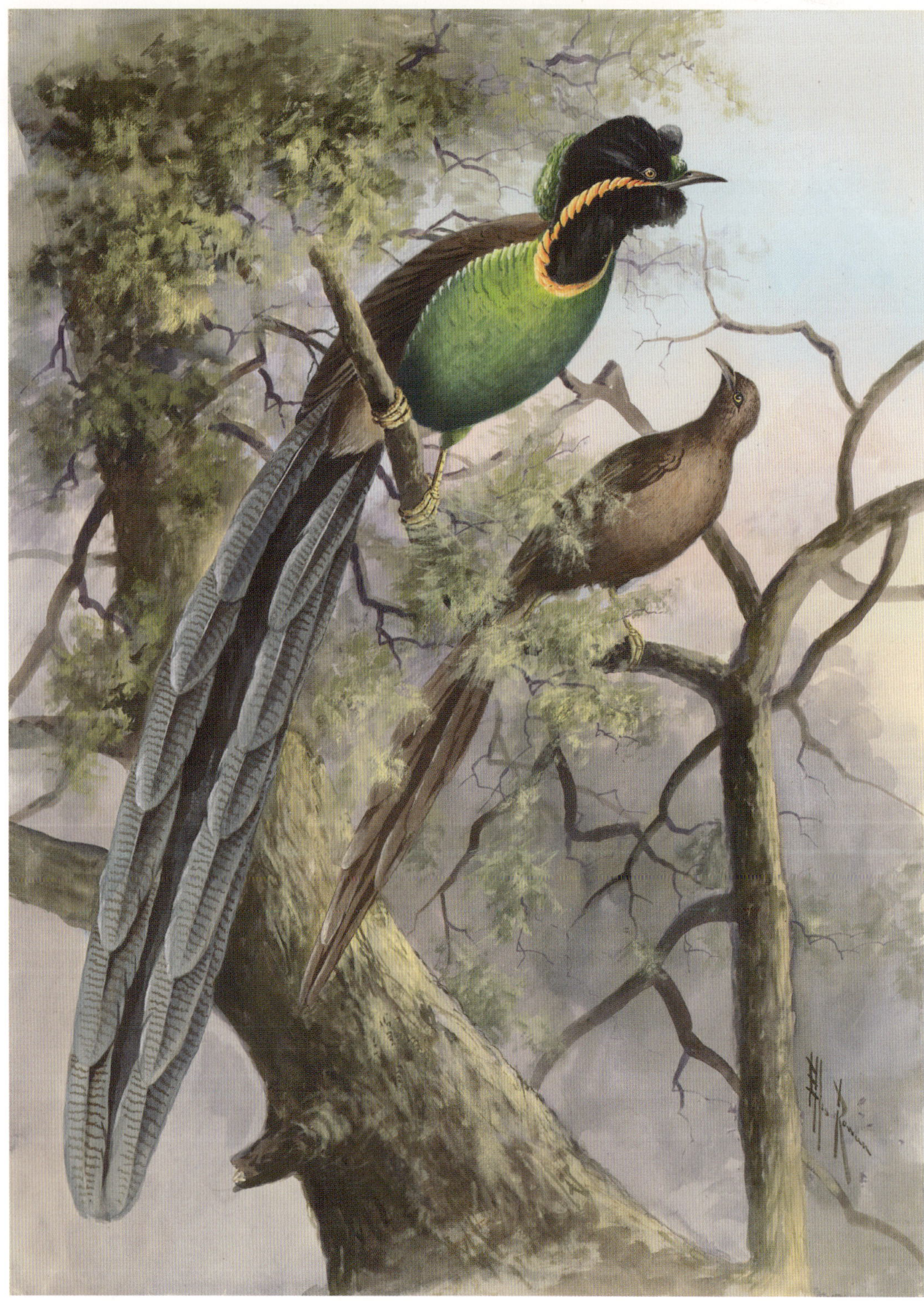

Rothschild's Bird of Paradise c.1917
gouache and watercolour on paper; 76.5 x 56.2 cm; Papua New Guinea
nla.cat-vn1165239